The Word of the Lord

The Word of the Lord

John R. Bisagno

BROADMAN PRESS
Nashville, Tennessee

ISBN: 0–8054–2221–8
Library of Congress catalog number: 72–96153
Printed in the United States of America

Contents

I How Much
Do I Have to Give? 7

II How Much
Do I Have to Do? 23

III What Do You Mean
—Believe? 39

IV What About
the Holy Spirit and Tongues? 51

V Why Doesn't God
Answer My Prayers? 73

VI What Do I Do
with My Sins? 87

VII What Does God
Expect from Me? 99

VIII Tell Me the Truth
About Demon Possession 111

IX What's Happening
to Our World? 129

I

How Much
Do I Have to Give?

Simply stated, three questions must be answered regarding the matter of the stewardship of our possessions. It is to be clearly understood and should go without saying that every good and perfect gift comes down from the Father. And all that we are and have is the result of his blessing. It is all his, and we are but stewards of what he has given us. Jesus spoke more about our relationship to our physical possessions than almost any other subject. Well did he speak and wisely when he said, "Where your treasure is, there will your heart be also." "Seek ye first the kingdom of God" and "Lay not up for yourselves treasures upon earth" are some of the wisest admonitions that ever fell from the lips of our Lord. No man can be properly related to God until he has properly related himself to those physical blessings which God has given him.

The three questions which each Christian must answer regarding his giving as a token of his love and gratitude to his heavenly Father are: How much am I to give? Where am I to give? For what purpose am I to give?

Let us look closely at what we learn from our own experience, from the Word of the Lord, and from the dictates of our own conscience, related to these three cornerstones of our giving.

1. *The percentage of our giving.* Every pastor has been asked by prospective church members, "Preacher, how

much will it cost me to be a member of your church?"
To which I always reply, "Everything you are, everything
you have, and everything you ever shall have." What a
pity it is that so little is required of the average church
member. It is far harder to become a member of the local
Rotary Club or Lions Club than most local churches.

When Jesus spoke in the Sermon on the Mount regarding the discipleship of our Christian responsibility,
he did not say, "If you decide to pray." He said, "When
you pray, enter into your closet." He did not say, "If you
choose to fast." He said, "When ye fast, do so with a
happy face." Nor did he say, "If you decide you would
like to give a little." He said, "Do so for the glory of God,
not the praise of man." In short, there was no option in
the mind of Jesus regarding a man's Christian responsibility in certain expected obligations and requirements.
It is not "if"; it is "when ye give, when ye fast, when ye
pray." It is not a question for discussion and considera-
tion. It is not an option and not a choice. It is a require-
ment expected by our Savior for those who would be his
disciples. It is all his. Everything is his, and he will have
us on no terms short of total surrender. Our Lord Jesus
was never intended to be simply a fire insurance policy
to keep the believer out of hell. To be sure, he does
rescue us from sin, death, hell, and the grave, but for
everytime he is called Savior, he is called Lord ten times.
He is to be Master, owner, controller, boss, Lord. And
it is only that kind of commitment to Christ which is the

genuine article. It is the nature of saving faith that it endures with total commitment.

An old country preacher used to say, "If your faith fizzles at the finish, it was faulty from the first." Let there be no question that it is all the Lord's. His to command, his to control as Lord of our lives. And yet, that answer alone is not satisfactory in the practical experiences of our daily stewardship.

In response to the question, "How much?" There must be a point of departure, a basis, a place to begin. That place is unquestionably: *The tithe is the Lord's. The tithe is holy unto the Lord. Bring ye all the tithes into the storehouse.*

Often it is argued we are not under the law, we are under grace. And yet, some things should be pointed out. Abraham tithed before the law, and Jesus commended men for tithing after the law. The counsels and purposes of God are changeless. His directives are irrevocable. While it is true that we are not under the law, it is equally true that we are above the law and that if the tithe was commanded under the law, how much more is that changeless blessing to be added to by the blood-bought child of God who is under love, under grace.

Our God never came to destroy one jot or tittle of the law. He came to fulfil it. Tithing is the very least we can do. Tithing acknowledges God as our financial partner and the administrator of our affairs.

Often people say to me: "Preacher, I can't tithe. I

don't make enough. I am behind in my bills and have more bills to pay than I have income." To which I say: "Man, you'd better tithe. You will never get out of that mess until you bring God in to perform some miracles!"

Our Lord could not have been plainer than when he said to the Pharisees regarding their tithing, "These things ought ye to have done." The literal rendition of the word "ought" is "must." It is imperative. This must be done! The tithe is holy unto the Lord. How much plainer could it be? He does not say 8 percent, or 12 percent, or 20 percent, but the 10 percent. It is there— plain, indisputable, and unchanging. The tithe is holy unto the Lord. (See Lev. 27:30.)

Notice the word *is*. It is the present tense of the verb *to be*. The tithe *is* the Lord's. Wherever it is, it is his. It may be on your back in the form of a new coat. You may be driving the Lord's tithe down the street in the form of your new car. You may be watching the Lord's tithe nightly in the form of a color TV set. You may be stealing it, robbing it, driving it, or wearing it. But, it is still not yours. It is his. The tithe is holy unto the Lord and then the tithe is *holy*. Not many things are called holy. But when something is set aside as being holy, it is dangerous to interfere with it or become involved with it in an unholy manner.

The ark of the covenant was holy and God forbade the ark to be touched. Uzzah touched the ark in insincerity and died. The vessels in the Temple were holy. Belshazzar touched them in insincerity and died as well. And, because it is the Lord's, when it is given to him, nothing is lost, but all is gained, for the giver is blessed in honoring God.

Early in my first pastorate, I learned well that the church that gives enhances evangelism. We were in the midst of perennial revival. On a particular Sunday Dr. T. B. Lackey, the executive secretary of our Oklahoma Baptist Convention, was invited to preach on the Cooperative Program. At the end of his message on giving, seventeen lost men and women accepted Christ as their personal Savior.

A church in its giving does not find that proper stewardship interferes with its own budget. At the close of the first revival I ever had in my church as a pastor, we gave our visiting evangelist over $4,000 in a love offering. My deacons expected that the church would surely go broke. The next Sunday we received the largest offering for our own local church offering in the history of our church. What had happened? Our people had learned the joy of giving, and after they had given to others, they continued to give to us as well. You simply can't outgive God. "Give," he says, "and it shall be given unto you; good measure pressed down, . . . and running over."

Tithing is the only directive in the Scripture I have found that can be tried on a trial basis. "Test me, try me, and prove me says the Lord, if I will not pour out a blessing you can not even contain!"

The Bible warns, "Will a man rob God?" I would sooner rob a bank than to rob God! And, to the individual I say again, the worse your financial condition, the more you need to tithe. Someone has well said that if your outgo exceeds your income, your upkeep will be your downfall. In a day in which many millions of Americans find themselves in an impossible financial dilemma, I urge you to take God at his word and begin giving him what is his. Slowly, but ever so surely, you will see that God will bless you and your financial picture will begin to change.

Often we object that the church is always pressuring us to give more money. Let me share with you a story. A deacon in a former pastorate told me of twin sons with which God had unexpectedly blessed him and his wife many years before. "When those boys were born, Preacher, we had no idea how we were going to afford them. Frankly I thought they were going to break us. There were two sets of school books to buy, always two dental bills and doctor bills, two tricycles, two Sunday suits. Then they went to college—two tuitions, two cars, two everything! It was so expensive. And, then one day, ever so unexpectedly, they died. Pastor," he sobbed, "since that day, they haven't cost us a dime."

Remember, the gospel is free, but it costs plenty to pipe it to the world. Yes, a church on the move, a strong evangelistic and missionary church is an expensive concern. But, the most expensive luxury in the world, and one which none of us can afford, is one that is doing nothing! That which costs nothing, accomplishes nothing, and is worth nothing. The Lord has a program for financing his work and it includes a blessing for the participants. The tithe is holy unto the Lord.

2. *The place of giving.* Where is the tithe to be brought? Our Lord has made it very clear that the percentage of giving is the tithe. We are told on the first day of the week that everyone is to lay by in store as God has prospered him. Two directives are very clear in this statement. First, there is a reaffirmation of percentage given. "As God has prospered him" makes giving equal. The millionaire and the less wealthy person are equal in their giving in relationship as God has prospered them. And, what is that relationship? that percentage? It is ten percent.

Secondly, the apostle Paul states that we are to bring it on the first day of the week. What happens on the first day of the week? Obviously, the local New Testament church is at worship. Paul further exhorts that we are not to forsake the assembling of ourselves together. To what assembly does he refer? The assembling on the first day of the week. Early in the Scriptures our Lord set the example for the sabbath day of rest and worship on the seventh day. But on that Calvary weekend something happened. Our Lord Jesus had died and was in the grave on Saturday. But on the first day of the week, when they came to embalm the body, the Lord had risen, and from

that point every stated example of New Testament worship was on the first day of the week in honor of the risen
Lord. Every time the resurrected Lord came into the
company of worshiping believers, honoring, blessing,
and approving their worship by his personal presence,
it was on the first day of the week. Obviously, we are not
to worship a dead Christ. Obviously, the tradition was
changed with the approval of the Lord Jesus to the first
day of the week. Naturally, unquestionably, it is to that
assembly on the first day of the week, the local worshiping New Testament church, that the tithe—stated in
Scripture, commended by the Lord Jesus, and practiced
to this day—was and is to be brought.

Notice that he has said, "Bring ye all the tithes," not
send them. For even in the act of bringing there is personal worship. They are to be brought weekly, not
monthly, or annually, or whenever possible, for it is a
part of our weekly stewardship in worship.

The word "church" in the New Testament refers 90
percent of the time to that local, first-day worshiping
body of baptized believers. Only 10 percent of the time
does it refer to the church-at-large, the body of Christ
worldwide. Until our Lord comes for his own and the last
soul for whom Christ died is brought into the fold, it will
be our responsibility to worship with and to tithe in and
through the local New Testament church.

Years ago, a woman applied for membership in the
Bellevue Baptist Church of Memphis, Tennessee, and

requested to sing in the choir. When her pastor, Dr. Lee, asked her where her membership was, she answered: "I don't belong to any church. I am a member of that great invisible church." "Well," Dr. Lee responded, "Why don't you go sing in that great invisible choir!"

It is not our privilege to scatter our tithe around to the Crusade for Christ, Youth for Christ, the Billy Graham Evangelistic Association, and a hundred other worthy causes that may receive offerings above the tithe. The tithe is to be brought into the body of worshiping believers the first Sunday—in short, the local New Testament church. By the way, don't sell the church short, friend; it will be here when the rest of them are dead and gone.

Any organization, any institution that does not originate in, work through, consumate in, exhault, edify, and honor the local New Testament church, will come to naught. There are many glamorous organizations today to which Christians are sending their tithes rather than to the local New Testament church. It may not happen today, tomorrow, next year, or twenty years from now, but mark my words, that institution, organization, or movement which is not in the middle of a New Testament church is destined to failure.

The YMCA was begun as a so-called "arm of the church" by evangelist Dwight L. Moody as a soul-winning organization for young men. But it is anything but that today. If there was a better way to do the work of the Lord on this earth than through the cooperation of the local New Testament churches, the Holy Spirit would have thought about it two thousand years ago.

You can not improve on what God has done. The place for your tithe is the church. And may I add that the church does not have to tithe to its mission boards. If a church gives 1 percent, 20 percent, 50 percent or 90 percent to missions, that's fine. There is no precedent for the church giving 10 percent to anything. The church does not pay tithes; it receives tithes. The tithe is the Lord's, and the church is the storehouse.

3. *The purpose for our stewardship.* No single book, let alone one closing point in a chapter, could exhaust what the redeemed child of God feels in his heart of love for his Lord Jesus in gratitude for his salvation. But let me suggest why we tithe. We tithe because it is commanded and love obeys. All through the Scriptures love is equated with action. Listen again to our Lord.

"Lovest thou me? Feed my sheep."

"Lovest thou me? Keep my commandments."

"For God so loved the world, that he gave . . ."

"Greater love hath no man than this, that a man lay down his life for his friends."

Love is no mere soupy sentimental attitude. It does not just sing, "Oh, how I love Jesus." It tithes. It does not simply feel, it does. Love is never equated with emotion in the Scripture but always with action. Love is something you do. Because the tithe is holy and it is commanded and it is his, we show our love in obedience.

We do not, we dare not, we must not touch what is God's.

The story is told that on a Jewish altar two doves were placed on a bed of live coals in sacrifice to God. Circling high above, two vultures eyed the dead birds. Hesitating at first, they were finally overcome with the selfish desire to take those birds to the nest of their young. Finally, one of the circling vultures swooped down and snatched the bird. Unknown to her, clinging precariously to the bottom of the dead dove was a live coal. Soon the offering was deposited high atop the mountain of her own sanctuary in the waiting beaks of her young. Within the hour, she returned to find her nest destroyed and her babies dead. She had stolen the Lord's sacrifice, and a live coal had clung thereto.

The tithe is holy. It is God's. There is a blessing when we give it and a curse when we steal it. You cannot win when you steal from God. We tithe because in obedience we obey our Lord. We give him what is rightfully his. I warn you. Don't touch the Lord's sacrifice! Further, we tithe because we love him. What more can be said of our love for our Friend of friends—our lovely Lord Jesus.

What does it mean to us when we think of our own salvation, of the price of that bloody cross, of heaven gained and hell spurned, of the worth of our own loved ones and the price paid for them. What price shall be placed on the value of a soul?

Many years ago in a small western Oklahoma farming

community, two college preacher boys had labored long and faithfully in the course of a two-week revival. At the business meeting which followed on Wednesday night, several of the people were complaining because the love offering of $1400 had been given the two young men, and only one young soul had been converted—a small lad of nine years.

A heated debate ensued, surrounding the matter of placing all future honorariums for revivals in the budget at a stipulated amount of $300, for that kind of money was just far, far too much for only one convert. Suddenly, dramatically, a tall Oklahoma wheat farmer strode to the front of the congregation, took out his checkbook and, as a tear dampened his cheek, said with trembling voice: "I want each of you people who complained here tonight to come down and tell me exactly what you gave and I will give you every penny back you put in the love offering. Yes," he said, "there was only one little boy saved in this revival, but that little boy was my little boy."

What price a soul? What price Calvary? Nothing we can do could ever compensate for what he gave for us when he bought my soul at Calvary.

> There is a cross for everyone to bear.
> There is a heartache for each soul to share.
> But, there is a place in Heaven waiting me,
> I got it through His death at Calvary.

Each drop of blood bought me a million years,
A soul was born each time He shed a tear.
I breathe His name each time I see a tree,
On which He bought my soul at Calvary.

The tithe is holy unto the Lord.

II

**How Much
Do I Have to Do?**

Ye have heard that it hath been said, An eye for an eye, and a tooth for a tooth: But I say unto you, that ye resist not evil: but whosoever shall smite thee on thy right cheek, turn to him the other also. And if any man will sue thee at the law, and take away thy coat, let him have thy cloke also. And whosoever shall compel thee to go a mile, go with him twain. Give to him that asketh thee, and from him that would borrow of thee turn not thou away. Ye have heard that it hath been said, Thou shalt love thy neighbour, and hate thine enemy. But I say unto you, Love your enemies, bless them that curse you, do good to them that hate you, and pray for them which despitefully use you, and persecute you (Matt. 5:38–44).

Has it ever occurred to you that while it is relatively easy to become a Christian, probably the most difficult thing in the world is to be a Christian. Obviously hundreds and thousands of persons have become Christians and are in the strictest sense of the word bonified Christians. They have had a conversion experience and have been saved. But, oh, the trouble they have living like Christians. There is, indeed, a big difference in becoming a Christian, which is very easy, and being a Christian, which is very difficult. While we are born of the spirit by divine operation by the Holy Spirit, we live out our life in a body of flesh. And to do physically what we know ideally to do is not nearly as easy as simply deciding to do it when first we receive Christ as personal Savior.

Jesus never made any apologies for the stringent demands he made upon his disciples. It costs something to be a Christian. It is a tough responsibility.

The expression "going the second mile" has become a part of the vernacular, of personality development, salesmanship, and positive living. But most people today do not know what Jesus was saying. For in the context of his day, the Jews of Palestine were a conscripted people. The Roman government had overpowered and enslaved them. The Roman legislature had imposed upon them many responsibilities. Some of them were easy—some of them were rather pleasant as a matter of fact, but this one in the minds of the proud Jewish people who were being suppressed and controlled by a foreign power was difficult and distasteful.

The law said that if a Roman soldier was carrying his pack and walking down a country road and he happened to come across a Jewish boy working in the field, or even an old man for that matter, that he had the right to compel that man to carry his pack for a mile. Hopefully, at the end of that mile he could find someone else he could compel to carry it another mile.

You can imagine the bombshell that Jesus dropped in the thinking of his people when he said that if any man, and he was specifically speaking about these Romans, compels you to go one mile, you cheerfully go with him a second mile. Not only were they to go by the law of the land, but "then some."

I can imagine that many a man and boy were barely able to make that mile and that only at the sacrifice of their own offended dignity! Perhaps a man was working in a field and fighting a deadline to get the harvest completed before the rains came. Suppose he was fighting a deadline to get his business completed in the marketplace before five o'clock, and he was so close. And, just a few minutes before five o'clock there came a Roman soldier into the marketplace and demanded that he stop what he was doing and carry his pack a mile. I suppose at the end of many such a journey more than one Hebrew boy had flung his pack at the feet of the Roman soldier and said, "I'll see you some night in a dark alley and get even for this." Many people take the demands of life just like that and say, "I'll do what I have to do whether I like it or not, but I'm not going to like a thing about it."

Can you imagine when one day a Roman soldier comes upon a boy in the field and demanding that he carry his pack a mile, the boy smiles and gladly carries it? As he walks, he says: "Tell me about the wonderful places you've been! Tell me about the great ocean. How do you like our people?" At the end of the mile the soldier notices that the boy is still happily walking along, talking and carrying the pack. As they are coming into the third mile, the soldier sees the boy is still enjoying himself. He is dumbfounded. He has never seen this dimension of living in anyone he has ever forced to carry out the law.

Somewhere down the road he gets to feeling kind of guilty and he says: "Son, I hate to tell you this, but you have gone a whole lot farther than that second mile and you really don't have to go this far." The boy says: "I have really enjoyed the walk, talking with you. I have just enjoyed knowing you. I belong to a new religion called 'The Way' and our Master taught us that as his followers we are supposed to do things like this. I found out a long time ago that if you do what Jesus says, it actually becomes rather pleasant. Come by again some time, I'd like to know you better." The Roman soldier goes off mumbling under his breath, and I wonder if somewhere down the line he might not have been that very soldier who fell down at the cross and said: "I never saw a man live or die like that man. Surely this was the Son of God."

Let me suggest three lessons from Jesus' teaching that if a man commands you to go one mile, you as a Christian, as a citizen of another world, abiding by different directions, marching to the beat of a different drummer, have an obligation and a blessing and privilege of not only going that one, but a second mile also.

1. I would suggest first of all to you that every man in life has the obligation of going that first mile. In a very real sense all of life can be categorized into two divisions—the first mile and the second mile, things that

come easy and things that come hard.

This word that Jesus used when he said if a man compel you to go a mile, go a second, is an old Persian word which means to conscript. It has in it a sense of binding constraint, a sense of forced regimented discipline. There is no question of release. It is there. It is a part of life. There are a lot of people in life who have never really grown to the mentally healthy state where they can accept things as they are. They are always trying to wiggle out of the basic responsibilities of life. To them I would suggest that life, by the very nature of the fact that you are alive and living in it, does have the right to demand some basic requirements of you.

Life certainly has the privilege of saying to us by the fact that we live in the blessed presence of some built-in blessings and benefits as being human beings, God's beautiful world has the right to charge us with some responsibilities. Lots of people have never come to understand that life really doesn't owe them all that much. But I owe my Lord, my church, my society, and my city—I owe life some things. This is a very simple and basic principle of life which Christian people need to be reminded of especially in the context of a life style that says: "I can get it for you wholesale," "You can make more by not working than by working," and "You get something for nothing, if you play all the angles." Well, the world really doesn't owe you nearly as much as you owe the world, as you owe your God and as you owe your church and your government.

The Bible doesn't say that we have to go to church on Wednesday night. There comes a time when you can choose what you will do in going that second mile or not, but the Bible very clearly says "do not forsake the assembling of yourselves together." There are some things that are required in being parents and good church members, in being good neighbors and in paying our bills, in obeying the law and in helping other people.

Far too many people do not understand that the first mile has the privilege of being extracted from us. You say: "Preacher, I just don't like that. I just don't like the fact that there are some laws and rules that are imposed on me for the good of society and some things that the Lord lays down on my life." Well, the Jews didn't like it either! But Jesus said to obey the laws of the land. He said that we are to render unto Caesar that which is Caesar's and unto God that which is God's and we will get a whole lot more done in life. Instead of being antagonistic, resentful, hateful, judgmental, and argumentative about everything in life, just grow up and understand that there are some things that are required in life whether we like it or not. We just can't go through life juicing out all of the goodies and all of the benefits without paying the restrictions that are imposed upon us by the first mile.

2. The second thing I would suggest to you is that the second mile begins where the first mile ends. A lot of

folks like to enjoy the pleasures of the second mile, but they don't want to pay the price of the first.

One girl went to college and stayed until she got nine years of straight *A*'s, but she had never gotten a degree because all she took was the electives. She enjoyed the electives and didn't want to take the requirements. If we are not careful, we will find that life offers so many glamorous electives of the second mile that we never fulfil the requirements.

It's kind of like the mother who told her son, "I want you to eat a little bit of spinach." And the boy responded, "How little can I eat?" You cannot enjoy any of the benefits of the second mile unless you have walked that first mile. It starts where the first one ends.

I suppose that every year about one hundred men in our church surrender to preach. And would you believe that about 90 percent of those feel led to be evangelists. They see Billy Graham preaching to thousands of people and Richard Hogue comes in with a big team and the church is packed and thousands are saved, and, boy, that's for them. Every young preacher that I talk to wants to be an evangelist. But too many don't want to drive clear across the country or hitchhike three or four hundred miles to preach in a one-room country schoolhouse, but they sure would like to hold a citywide revival. I found a long time ago that if you don't go that first mile of the discipline of college and seminary and be faithful over the little opportunities, you will never have the chance to be faithful over much. You can't go that second mile until you have fulfilled the first. The first mile is the hard one. It is what is demanded and required of us. I don't believe that God is going to bless you with the promised blessings in that second mile until you have first fulfilled the requirements of the first.

Someone asked me the other day what I thought about hippies. We have some hippies in our church and they are loved and wanted. But I notice there are a lot of people in this world who put down the establishment who don't mind taking the establishment's penicillin, don't mind hitchhiking rides in the establishment's cars, enjoying the establishment's society, wearing the establishment's clothes, or going to the establishment's door to get a dollar for a frankfurter or a fix. All they want to do is enjoy the benefits of the second mile, and let society pay the requirements of the first.

Our church supports many, many wonderful causes. Sometimes it is very easy for us to give money to Billy Graham, Campus Crusade, and Youth for Christ. And many of us are concerned that some of these organizations don't go under financially. But you must be concerned, first of all, that the church stay afloat. That is your first responsibility. Some of us like to give our time and work in some of the more exciting phases of the ministry. And that's good, but not at the sacrifice of our responsibility to our church.

Dr. Criswell said recently that for the first time in history the First Baptist Church of Dallas was facing some serious financial curtailment of their ministry because many of their people were giving to all of the glamorous things instead of giving their time and tithe through their local church. It is so easy for us to let this attitude which permeates society sneak into the church and let the glamorous things in the second mile substitute for the responsibilities of the first. I say to you that we have no right to expect the benefits that come in that second mile until we accept the responsibility that is in our tithes, our work, and our attendance in the church for which Jesus died. We must keep priorities in place. If we don't, the benefits of the first will be thwarted and there won't *be* any second mile or third! I have noticed that not very many people are ever invited to sing in our church who are not choir members. I like that. Many people come because they want to be the star. We want the blessing of the second mile and the great benefits of being a fine soloist, but we don't want to come to choir practice two or three hours every week. That's the way it should be. The blessing of the second mile is to be found only at the end of the first.

3. The third word is this—the greatest blessings of life are to be found in that second mile. Jesus said in Matthew 16:25, "Whosoever will save his life shall lose it." This means that the man is self-possessive whose attitude toward life is me, mine, I'll get mine first, I'll look out for old number one. That man is going to end up

losing the very thing he is trying to save. But, "whosoever will lose his life for my sake shall find it." At the end
of life, you will find, that the only things you have kept
are those things you have given away in the service of
the dear Lord to other people.

Jesus told Peter to forgive not seven times, "but seventy times seven." Now Jesus was not limiting to 490 the
times that you are to forgive. He was saying indefinitely,
always, you keep on forgiving. The man who is always
keeping score of what the world owes him, how many
times he has been offended, and how many times he has
had to forgive, that man is always going to have a personality that is crippled, pitiful, and little.

The Pharisees had it all figured out that if you didn't
commit the physical act of adultery you were safe, but
you could think all you wanted. Jesus said, to be sure,
that the restrictions of the first mile are irrevocable.
Adultery is still not to be committed. The sabbath is still
to be kept holy. The tithe is still holy unto the Lord. But
Jesus said that the man who lives in the area of the
second mile is not under the law—he is above the law
and if the law demands 10 percent, how much more will
he gladly give because he is above the law. The law says
thou shalt not commit the act. He says I want you to
understand that the blessing lies in the second mile. We
are not to grudgingly refuse to do the act, but to do so
gladly in our hearts.

Ours is always a second-mile religion. Therein lies the

blessing. These disgruntled keepers-of-the-law were the most miserable folk in the world. I know of nothing more miserable than a church member who says, "I'll tithe, but I don't want to."

I think of our deaf people who could stay at home and grumble and gripe at God and say, "Why have you made me deaf?" What a blessing they are to thousands of people because they go above and beyond with what they have to do, having fulfilled the responsibility of that first mile, having been loyal to God, not having griped to God, they have gone a step further and even praised God in the second mile. They see an opportunity in everything that they do to praise God.

I think of that deacon coming when he doesn't have to—when he is as tired as anyone else—and saying: "Preacher, don't worry about some little problem, forget about it, we will take care of that." It is that Sunday School teacher who doesn't have to be there until everyone else does, but who comes early because he wants to be more than ready. These teachers want to have their hearts ready and the room ready, they want that extra dimension of their very earliness to say to that class member, "We really do love you and want you." It is that committee member or church member who, in some decision of the church, finds himself in the minority, responding to the unwritten code of love which says: "Though I may disagree, I will not be disagreeable. And, whether I have my way or not, though it is my right to oppose on the floor of the church and call all my friends and to gossip in the halls, I will forego that right. I will be a contributing part of the solution rather than a part of the problem and will try to convince everyone else to follow the dictates of the majority of the church." Now, that translated into Monday, Tuesday, and Wednesday action is a little bit of what Jesus meant when he talked about going the second mile.

In the East it is said there was a grand and famous surgeon. A young doctor came and watched him do his surgery and greatly benefited therefrom. One day some of the young men began to notice that at the end of every operation rather than simply tying two knots the doctor had a habit of tying three knots. At the end of one of his operations, a young student said: "I notice you follow the book right to the letter. You made the incision like the book said, you brought the veins together like the book said. And the book says when you finish the operation to tie two knots. Is that right?" "Yes, that's what the book says," answered the doctor. "I don't understand," the student said. "Will you please explain?" The doctor said, "Son, that's my sleeping knot." The boy asked what was a sleeping knot. "Every day life is placed precariously in my hands. I go home at night, and time after time I redo in my mind each step of that operation to see if I have made a mistake. Sometimes when I am tired and worried and can't sleep, I always look back and remember that I have done it right and I put the frosting on the cake. I tied not only that knot properly but a second and a third knot, and I just smile and go back to sleep. The third one is my sleeping knot!"

If our attitude of life is so self-centered that we will do just what life demands if it kills us and no more, we will never experience the blessing of that second mile. If we try to substitute the joy of the second mile without the restrictions of the first, we shall equally fail to profit thereby. When we have gladly gone the distance of the first mile and then because our attitude has been beautiful and happy we have walked into the second mile, we shall find there the choice blessings of life await from him who said: "If a man compel you to go a mile, go with him twain."

III
**What Do You Mean
—Believe?**

"When he was in Jerusalem at the passover, in the feast day, many believed in his name, when they saw the miracles which he did. But Jesus did not commit himself unto them, because he knew all men" (John 2:23–24).

Can you imagine a preacher getting up a crowd like Jesus had that day? Jerusalem was not only the most important, but the largest city in the country. The Feast of the Passover was the most important religious holiday, and people came literally from all over that part of the world and they came by the tens of thousands. The Lord Jesus was riding the crest of popularity and thousands were following him, hearing, and responding to his invitation. I cannot help but believe that more people came forward on the invitation to follow Christ at this point than any point in the earthly ministry of Jesus.

But Jesus turned and fled to the mountains. He did not have them fill out any cards. He did not counsel with them. He said: "No, you don't understand. You have missed the point of why I have come." They responded to him, but Jesus did not commit himself to them. Can you imagine a preacher giving an invitation to ten thousand people and three thousand coming forward and the preacher telling them to go back to their seats? They believed in him, but he did not commit himself unto them. Strange. The word "believe" and the word "commit" are the identical same term. Why did he not believe

in them? Because they believed for a shallow reason.
They believed because of the show. They believed because of the excitement. They saw the miracles that he
did—he fed thousands, and raised the dead. It was popular to be a Christian. Everyone was walking down the
aisles and following Jesus. And he fled and said: "Go
back. You don't understand. You have missed it."

A lot of people miss it. Jesus was talking about dying,
death, crucifixion. Talking about commitment to a cross.
And, Peter said: "No. Far be it, Lord. It will not be so."
Jesus said: "Get thee behind me, Satan. You are an
abomination to me." Peter had no concept of the death
of Christ or the death of self. It was all what was in it for
him, and he missed what it was to make a commitment.

The evangelist comes to town, the church is packed,
people come forward. They come back on Wednesday
night and the preacher starts talking about visitation,
about tithing, soul winning, death to self, and Wednesday night goes down to a pitiful few. Why? Because they
believed for the wrong reason. They were following him
for the show. For the excitement, and the spotlight and
thrill of the crowd and the zest, zing, and sensation.

Many believed on him when they saw the miracles, not
when they heard what he said. I don't think they were
hearing what he was saying. It was only when they saw
the show that they believed. But Jesus did not believe in
them. This word "commitment" is the one best word
that means to be a Christian. I submit to you that the

Bible actually tells a lot of things to a lot of different people to be saved. Jesus said to one man, "You must be born again." He said to another man, "Go sell all your goods and give them to the poor." He told another man to "repent." The fact is that all of these things are simply saying that whatever is standing in the way of the totality of your commitment to Jesus Christ must be dealt with because that is what it means to be a Christian.

You understand that the Bible talks about believing in Jesus Christ. "God so loved the world, that he gave his only begotten Son, that whosoever believeth in him should not perish, but have everlasting life." It comes back again and says, "Thou sayest thou believest," and in sarcasm adds, "Thou doest well. Devils also believe and tremble." So, obviously, there are two kinds of faith. There are two kinds of commitment. There are two kinds of what it means to believe in Jesus Christ. Sometimes folks come down the aisle and profess to be saved, put on a good act, and may even stick with it for five years or even ten or twenty. But eventually they backslide and start living like the devil again and go away from God and forget the whole thing, and folks just assume that they have lost their salvation, that they are lost and are going to hell. They are going to hell, not because they lost their salvation, but because they never had it in the first place.

To believe means to make an irrevocable commitment. It means to keep on believing, endlessly. When I stop believing, I prove that I never had saving faith at all. In other words, it is the nature of New Testament saving faith that it makes a commitment and starts believing and never stops believing. When a man stops believing, when he terminates that commitment, he proves that he never had it in the first place because saving faith doesn't give up its commitment. It can't. The other kind of belief is a show and a sham and it is not the real article.

The Bible says, "Whosoever is born of God does not commit sin." To commit means to give in totality—"over to." When someone is committed to an institution, they are put there permanently. They are committed. It doesn't mean a man will never fall into sin. But, it means that the man who is genuinely born of God cannot give a committal back again over to a life-style of sin, because the new seed of saving faith is in him and he cannot make that recommittal over to sin.

One of the things that really alarms me as I compare my Sunday morning crowd and my Wednesday night crowd is that God nowhere in the Bible lowers the standard or shortcuts what it means to be a Christian. He never substitutes quantity for quality. He is only looking for quality. Time and time again Jesus flees from the great numbers—he runs from the quantity and he looks deep into the heart for the depth of the quality of those who want to follow him.

You remember how Gideon's army was selected. There were thousands and thousands of soldiers who wanted to fight. God said to Gideon, "Let them have a simple little test." So they went down to the river and began to drink and of those who just jumped in and started to drink he said, "Send them back." But, of those who got a drink and kept looking for the enemy, those who really were committed to the job at hand, he said, "We'll use that three hundred." Thousands went back, and he chose the three hundred because God is not looking for quantity. He never substitutes quantity for quality.

You remember how in Sodom and Gomorrah two entire cities were destroyed and one person was saved while the populations of two of the world's great cities were destroyed in an instant. Why? Because God didn't love two cities? No. Because God never substitutes quantity for quality.

I remember that one day Jesus Christ fed five thousand people along with preaching his sermon. It was time for the all-church picnic and five thousand showed up to hear him preach his sermon! Then one day Jesus announced that he was going to preach but he wasn't going to feed. The crowd dropped to five hundred. Then Jesus said, "I want us to go aside and pray." The crowd dropped to a hundred and twenty. Then Jesus says: "This Monday night, fellows, it is time for citywide church visitation, and we are going to go by twos and witness to the ends of the earth," and the crowd drops down to seventy. Then he says: "I want some of you to follow me and be my personal disciples and friends. I want you to be on call day and night. I want you to be my own, my disciples, my strength, my help." The crowd drops to twelve. Then Jesus says: "I am going to ask us to go into the garden and there I am going to pray about a life and death matter of the kingdom of God which will cost my life and maybe yours." The crowd drops to three. Then one day Jesus said, "I am going to go to the cross to die." And, of the five thousand who were there when he fed and preached, and the five hundred who were there when he preached only, and of the hundred and twenty who were at the prayer meeting, and of the seventy who visited, and out of that small group of twelve who were on commitment day and night, and of the three who went into the garden to pray, only one disciple, *just one,* followed Jesus Christ all the way to the foot of the cross. Just one. John!

Sometimes people ask, Why was so much given to John more than all the other disciples? Why John? Many of the others were martyred, some were crucified. But, John lived to a ripe old age. Why? How was it that to John at the cross the Lord Jesus committed the care and the keeping of his own beloved mother. Why John? Why was it on the Isle of Patmos that God gave to John the beautiful vision of that escatological development of events, of all the things to come and all the things that would be. Why was it of all the Gospels John was permitted to write this beautiful wrap-up to the other Gospels, the Gospel of John? Why John? I don't know. But, I do know this. Out of the five thousand who ate, and five hundred who listened, and one hundred twenty who prayed, and seventy who visited, of the twelve who followed, and the three who prayed, only one, John, followed Jesus all the way to the cross. Does it pay to serve Jesus? Ask John. Commitment. That's what it means to be a Christian.

To far too many people Jesus Christ is a Sunday morning fire insurance policy to keep them out of hell and no more! I call your attention to the fact that every time he is called Savior, he is called Lord eleven times. Now what does the word "Lord" mean? In our vocabulary it means one word—boss. It means master, controller, owner, ruler. Boss! Jesus Christ is no fire insurance policy. That's what it means to be a Christian. It doesn't mean to argue with him. Sometimes people want to argue about being baptized. But I have found that you can hardly keep a real convert out of the baptistry. You see, there is a commitment that is irrevocable, for Jesus is Lord and Jesus is boss.

How about your commitment? Are you really a follower of Jesus Christ? I don't mean just on Sunday morning and Sunday night—I mean is a Monday night football game, a big sales deal, a play, a club meeting, or anything in this world as important as your commitment to Christ and his bride?

When Jesus Christ lives in the believer, he walks with him and lives in him. He uses the believer's eyes and tongue, hands, feet, and body. "Christ liveth in me. I am crucified. Nevertheless I live. Yet, not I, Christ." That is what it means to be a Christian—commitment to Christ!

Years ago I was in a revival in the city of McAllen, Texas. We were in the football stadium, and because I need all the help I can get in attracting a crowd, we had Ethel Waters one night and Tom Landry one night and this one and that one all giving their testimonies, and it was glorious. The people were coming and were being saved. On Thursday night we were to have a man named Jerry Stovall, linebacker for the St. Louis Cardinals football team. We went out to the airport to pick Jerry up. He had on a nice business suit with a briefcase, Bible, and a big grin. But over one shoulder was the ugliest looking old Army duffel bag you ever saw. After a bit I said: "Jerry, what is in your duffel bag? Are you going to give us a demonstration on how to be a linebacker?" He said, "No, those are my training clothes." I said, "Are you going on to training camp or something?" He said, "No, I'm going back to St. Louis." "You mean you brought them just for tonight?" "Yes, just for tonight."

I went to my room about six o'clock and had prayer and rested a little bit and got ready for church. About six-thirty I heard this strange sound outside my window. Sure enough there was Jerry in his sweat clothes jogging to town! I said, "Jerry, where are you going?" He said:

"I am going four miles. I'll be back in a minute." I was impressed.

That night he gave his testimony and then we returned to the motel. About ten o'clock I heard that knocking outside my window again. There was Jerry running for all he was worth. (And the next morning he did the very same thing). When I asked him why he ran twelve miles a day, he answered that he had been doing that for the last seventeen years. A nearby friend said, "Remember, he is an all-pro." I asked Jerry how long he had played football, and he said, "thirteen years." I asked him how long he had been an all-pro linebacker, and he timidly answered, "All thirteen years." That's commitment.

There are hundreds, thousands, tens of thousands, yes, and even millions in this world who are doing nothing but fooling themselves, thinking they are Christians but who have no commitment. To be a Christian means, pure and simple, making a commitment to the command, and control, and lordship of Jesus Christ. I demand in the name of Jesus Christ that you examine your commitment to Him.

You say, "I love the Lord, Preacher, but as far as coming to church all the time—no! I love Jesus but not the church." Jesus is the head of the bride. When you ignore Jesus' bride, you break his heart. When you insult his church you insult his bride. You hurt him. That's like saying you love swimming, but hate the water. You love eating, but not the food. You love music, but not the sound thereof. As the leaf is to the limb, the sunset is to the west, and the sap to the tree, so is the bride, the church, the body, the head, to the living Christ. Our commitment is to Christ, the head, and to her, his body.

IV

**What About
the Holy Spirit and Tongues?**

In my opinion, it is unfortunate that the name Holy Ghost ever was introduced into the old English manuscripts. In the interpretation of the Bible, the word "ghost" has a spooky connotation. He is called the comforter, counselor, the Holy Spirit, Spirit of the Ages, Holy Ghost—he has many different names; but he is one person to whom we shall refer hereafter as the Holy Spirit. Then, let it be understood that he is not something. He is someone. He is not to be called it. We err when we pray, "Lord, send the Holy Spirit, let it come." You would not introduce your wife as, "This is my wife, isn't it pretty?" "This is my son, isn't it nice?" You call a thing it, but a person is he. You insult the Holy Spirit when you call him it. He is not something; he is someone.

The Holy Spirit is personality. He is not just the spirit of '76 or like the spirit of a football game or the spirit of optimism or the spirit of influence, but a spirit of personality. He is somebody. He is someone. We must understand that we err when we ask the Holy Spirit to come among us. He does not come among us. He is not a commuter. He does not live out in space somewhere, for your body is the temple, as a Christian, of the Holy Spirit. When you are saved, he comes into your life. He lives in you. He indwells you. He never ever leaves. He may be grieved and quenched into one corner of your heart, but this divine person never leaves. If he did, you would be lost and before you could be saved again you would not have to come simply trotting down the aisle. You would have to live in fulfilment of Hebrews 6—a hypothetical case which says it is impossible, if a man could fall away, to ever renew him again to repentance. To do so the Lord Jesus would have to come from heaven, be born of hundreds of years prophecy, be born of a virgin, live a perfect life, and die again on the cross. Once for all he forever sat down at the right hand of the Father after he died for the sins of the world. The Spirit never leaves after salvation.

The Holy Spirit is God. He is not a representative of God. He is not an ambassador of God. He is not sent from God. He *is* God. Often times it is suggested that Christians have three Gods. Not so. We have one God who manifests himself in three different forms. In that form of creatorship and judgeship, controller and sustainer of the universe, it is as the Father. Sometimes he comes in visible form, and not just at Christmas. You recall that the Bible says when Shadrach, Meshach, and Abednego were thrust into the fiery furnace and the door was opened, there was a fourth man with them like unto the Son of God. There were many preincarnate, physical manifestations of Jesus Christ called the angel of the Lord and other names in the Old Testament. Our Lord, when he reveals himself so that we can see him, is as Jesus Christ. In the beginning was the word, logos, the mind, the image, the manifestation of God. When I say to you, "love," "father," "football," I am expressing to you what is in my mind, and until I make that tangible you do not know what I am thinking under the surface. We did not know what God was like, for God was invisible; therefore, he made himself tangible so that, just as a word could express the tangibility of what one is, we could comprehend what God was—that logos, that word was Jesus Christ.

Now sometimes God comes to the earth in invisible form and that is as the Holy Spirit. Understand that we only have one God. H_2O is only H_2O. Sometimes it is in solid form as ice. Sometimes it is in liquid form as water or in vaporous form as steam. But it is always H_2O. There is only one H_2O, but sometimes it is in three different forms. There is only one God and his name is Jehovah. But sometimes he exists in three different forms as Father, Son, and Holy Spirit. The Father, the Son, and the Holy Spirit are coeternal. They have always been. The Bible says, "In the beginning was the Word, [the logos, the Christ] and the Word was with God, and the Word was God." He existed with the Father and the Holy Spirit before the foundation of the world. The Bible tells us in Genesis 1:1 "In the beginning God created the heaven and the earth." The literal rendition of the Hebrew word interpreted "God" is "gods," for the Father, the Son, and the Holy Spirit worked in cooperation to create life. God never creates apart from the joint work of his word and his spirit. There must be the word and Spirit to bring forth life. He said, "Let it be." His word was attested to by the power of the Spirit and Christ, by whom all things are brought into existence. The word of the Father, the creation of the Son, the breath of the Spirit. Just so, there must be the word, the logos, the word which must be heard and understood, attested to by, convicted by, interpreted by, made distinct, be comprehensive by the Holy Spirit. And so, there is no stair-stepping in the Trinity. It is not the Father, then the Son, the servant of the Father, and then the Spirit, the servant of both. There is no stair-stepping in their authority. They are coequal.

In the Old Testament God appeared to Moses in physical form. Moses saw God, he talked to him, he sensed his presence and said, "Who are you?" And God said, "My name is I AM." Moses said, "Whom shall I say hath sent me when I do your work?" God said, "Say 'I AM' hath sent thee." He is always in the present tense. There is no yesterday, today, or tomorrow with him. He is always here, today. He is just AM. You cannot properly say he always was or he always will be. There are no limitations of time with God. He exists in eternity where the bounds of time do not exist. And only once in thirty-three years he stepped into the empirical realm where the bounds and boundaries of time do exist. You cannot say God always was or always will be. He is always in the present tense. The only way you can really say it is this: God "am" always been, he "am" right now, and he "am" always going to be. He just "am!" There are no limitations of time, no stair-stepping of authority. One God, who deals and reveals with men in three ways—always in the present tense.

When Jesus Christ was on this earth, it was in physical form we could touch, handle, see, relate to, and identify with. Now the Holy Spirit is here in invisible form, and our relationship to God is our relationship to the Holy Spirit who is God. Let me make that very clear. There is no matter more important in your life to be resolved than your relationship to God. And that is determined precisely by your relationship to the Holy Spirit, because that is the form through which God is dealing with us in this dispensation of time, in invisible form as the Holy Spirit, as he dwelt with men in visible form as Jesus for thirty-three years and primarily in his form as the Father before that time. This is the age of the Holy Spirit and this is the way God deals with us.

Our relationship to God is absolutely determined by our relationship to the Holy Spirit. He is God among us. He deals with us today through the invisible medium of the Holy Spirit.

What then, are the possible relationships to the Holy Spirit? What relationships can a person have to the Holy Spirit? How can we deal with him? I suggest to you that there are three possibilities.

First, it is possible to insult the Holy Spirit. Understand that to insult the Holy Spirit is to commit the unpardonable sin. It is that sin for which men can never be forgiven. It is not possible for the believer to commit it. If you are saved, you have passed from death unto life; you cannot commit the unpardonable sin. The unsaved person commits the unpardonable sin. To blaspheme the Holy Spirit is the unpardonable sin. Matthew 12:31 says, "Wherefore I say unto you, All manner of sin and blasphemy shall be forgiven unto men: but the blasphemy against the Holy Ghost shall not be forgiven unto men."

What does blasphemy mean? Blasphemy means to insult something sacred. I could go into a church one night, roll back the carpet, have a dance, write obscene words on the wall, and throw a drunken party. I would be insulting the building, but I would not be commiting the unpardonable sin. I could take the name of God in vain, but that is not the unpardonable sin. I could blaspheme and insult Jesus Christ, but that is not the unpardonable sin. I can take the utensils of the Lord's Supper table and get drunk in them, but that is not the unpardonable sin. But you cannot insult the Holy Spirit and be forgiven.

What is the Holy Spirit in the world to do? To the believer, many things. He guides me; he speaks to me; he fills me; he controls me; he comforts me; and he convicts me. But with an unsaved person: "When the Holy Spirit shall come," said Jesus, "he will testify of me. He will convict the world of sin, righteousness, and judgment." The Holy Spirit has one job with the unsaved person and that is to draw him to Jesus Christ.

Every time you go to church or hear a steeple bell ring, every time you hear a sermon, get a tract, turn on a service on TV—every time something happens that makes you even slightly aware of the fact you need to receive Jesus and be saved, that's the Holy Spirit. Only he can make that awareness. And to perpetually harden your heart so that you continually say no to drive the Holy Spirit away, to crucify the Holy Spirit, to rebel against him, to insult him by refusing to let him do the only thing he is in the world to do—that is to blaspheme the Holy Spirit. You insult him. You turn him away. You say: "Go Spirit, go thy way. I am not ready for you. I will be saved when I want to." No you won't. The Bible says, "My Spirit will not always strive with man." Three times in the first chapter of Romans the Bible says that God gave them up. God gave them up. God gave them up! Jesus said, "Except the Father that sent me draw him, no man can come." You won't be saved when you want. You will be saved when he wants. And it is not necessarily a great emotional experience.

When you are asked, "Do you intend to be saved one day?" and you answer yes you are under conviction. Only the Holy Spirit can give you that awareness. Many people do not have that awareness and cannot acknowledge that. They have no comprehension of their need of Christ. The unpardonable sin means to insult the Holy

Spirit, and to insult the Holy Spirit means to insult him by refusing to let him do the one thing he is in the world to do and that is to draw you to Jesus. The unpardonable sin is clearly blasphemy against the Holy Spirit. It is not just speaking against him, but insulting him by the hardening of your heart.

Verse 32 of Matthew 12 goes on to add something to what has been said. It has been clearly said that blasphemy against the Holy Spirit cannot be forgiven. But verse 32 adds, "whosoever speaketh against the Holy Ghost"—that cannot be forgiven either. For a man who speaks against him would have already blasphemed in his heart. The unpardonable sin is in the heart. The mouth is the fruit, but the heart is the root. He shows with his mouth what he has done in his heart, but he does not have to show it with his mouth. If he does, that it is only further evidence that it is an insulting rejection of the Spirit's call. People often commit the unpardonable sin in places like Texas, Mississippi, Alabama—the Bible Belt where more gospel is preached per square inch than anywhere in this world. You say, "What about the heathen in Africa who haven't heard? I say, "What about you in the United States who have heard a thousand times?" It is possible to insult the Holy Spirit and say no, leave me alone, I am not ready, maybe tomorrow, tomorrow, tomorrow, until God says, "Leave him alone!" You cannot insult the Spirit forever. If you drive him away, he will leave you.

The unpardonable sin is not just committed against the Holy Spirit's call to Jesus because he is the greatest but because he is the latest. He is the last. There is no other one coming. There is no other way. This is the last dispensation, the last stage, the last day. God has no other way of attracting men to Jesus than by giving them the awareness by the Spirit in their heart that they need to be saved. When you reject that, when you drive him away, you leave yourself locked in your sins. I plead with you to understand that it is dangerous to insult the Holy Spirit.

Secondly, one who is a believer can injure the Holy Spirit. The Holy Spirit simply lives in clean bodies, in clean minds, and clean hearts. At the risk of sounding blunt, frank, and crude, let me simply say to you that if you, as a believer, continue to live in sin and filth and refuse to get right, God will honor his word to you to keep you saved, but he will kill you, he will take your life, he will take you out of this world prematurely, so that he can keep his covenant. Oh, you will still be saved and go to heaven, but you will be taken prematurely. It is possible to commit what is called a sin unto death. First John 5:16, "If any man see his brother sin a sin which is not unto death, he shall ask, and he shall give him life for them that sin not unto death." Pray for your brother who sins a certain category of sins. But there is a type of sin which leads to death. I do not say that he shall pray for it, for that category of sin. What category is that?

In 1 Corinthians 5, the Bible tells the story about a man who was living in incest with his mother or stepmother. Paul says to turn that man over to the devil "for the destruction of the flesh, so the spirit might be saved in the day of the Lord Jesus." Kill him. Take him out of the way. Take him out of the world." More than one Christian living in overt sexual sins and immorality blatantly and flagrantly in the face of God has been killed.

A life that is a lie to the Holy Spirit is also in danger of being killed. Ananias and Sapphira were leaders in the church. There was a great revival going on, and it was embarrassing because everyone was giving a big offering; and Ananias and Sapphira were tight and stingy and on the spot. They did not want to give, but they had to give. The book of Acts tells us that they piously came forth and said: "We are going to give a great big offering. Here is our big offering. This is all we have. This is the money from some land that we sold to give money to the church." But, they really received a lot more, and God killed them on the spot. The Spirit of God killed them and they fell dead because their lives, as leaders in the church were a lie to the Holy Spirit. It is a dangerous thing to take up the offering, to sing in the choir, or to teach a class, to play the piano, to pass out the bulletins, or to touch and handle the things of God and your life be full of sin, your life be a lie to God. That is dangerous.

A sin unto death can be committed when a man twists the Scriptures to justify his own sins. Second Peter tells us about people who wrest, meaning to twist or to pervert Scriptures to justify their own sins. The Bible says that they do so to their own destruction. Once I had a friend who had two serious heart attacks. He never went to church. He lived like the devil and claimed to be saved. I said: "Man, you are flirting with death. You had better get right with God and get back to church." He said: "Oh, you know what we Baptists believe—once saved, always saved." He was dead in three days. You see, he was using the Scripture to justify his sin. Paul said, "Shall a man continue in sin that grace may abound?" God forbid.

The Corinthian church was getting drunk at the Lord's Supper table. They were unworthily handling the things of God. They were teaching lessons, singing in the choir, and using the Lord's Supper table and the vessels and the cup and the tray, and getting drunk and laughing about it and God killed them. Paul said that for this reason some are sick among you and some even sleep, some are dead, some have been killed.

I want to say to you that our God is a God of love and peace, but the gospel is a two-edged sword. God is also a God of harsh judgment. There is a line drawn and there are limitations set beyond which men may not go.

So, first, it is possible for us to insult the Holy Spirit. The unsaved person can drive him away in his refusal and pride to let him do the one thing he is in the world to do—to draw a person to Christ. The unsaved person runs the risk of committing the unpardonable sin.

Secondly, the believer can injure the Holy Spirit by having a body and a mind that is a lie of hypocrisy, filled with filth in which the Holy Spirit will refuse to dwell, so he leaves him and the man dies.

The third and final possibility of our relationship to the Holy Spirit is that you as a believer can experience him. To experience the Holy Spirit, to be filled, and controlled, and possessed by the Holy Spirit is the most beautiful, godly, imperative, and important part of life. You are made as a believer to be controlled by the Spirit. The body is made to be flooded and led by the Holy Spirit. As we talk about being filled with the Holy Spirit, let's get a couple of terms straight. People say to me sometimes, "Have you had the baptism?" I say: "Yes, I have had the baptism. Right after I was saved, I went to the baptistry and was baptized." "That's not what I mean," they say, "have you got the real baptism?" I reply, "What baptism?" "Have you had the baptism of the Holy Spirit?" I say, "No, I don't have that." They say, "Oh, you have got to get that." So I ask them to show me in the Bible where it says you have got to get it, and they can't do it. You cannot find this expression in the Scriptures. You cannot find the expression "baptism *of* the Holy Spirit" in the New Testament. It is not there. The Bible does have two other prepositions it does use. It says, "Ye shall be baptized *with* the Holy Spirit." Jesus told his disciples they would be baptized with the Holy

Spirit not many days hence.

And *that* prophecy was fulfilled on the day of Pentecost. They were baptized with the Holy Spirit—endued, saturated, annointed by him at Pentecost.

Then the Bible talks about being baptized *by* the Holy Spirit. Paul tells us that when a man is converted, he is baptized, introduced, injected *by* the Spirit into oneness with Jesus Christ. The Holy Spirit is the regenerating agent. It is he who introduces us into oneness with Jesus Christ. He merges our personality into that of Jesus, and that of Jesus into us. He is the agency of salvation. He is the one who brings about the regenerative process by which the personaiity of Christ is engrafted into the heart of the believer. But the Bible speaks nothing about the baptism *of* the Holy Spirit.

After a man is saved and is baptized by the Holy Spirit into oneness with Christ, there are many fillings of the Holy Spirit. Let's keep the terminology straight. Let's drop that "Have you got the baptism of the Holy Ghost?" for I don't and neither do you and neither does anyone else—there is no such thing! It simply is not in the Scriptures.

But the Bible does talk about being filled *with* the Holy Spirit. The command to be filled with the Holy Spirit is a continuous one, we are to keep on being filled, on and on, minute by minute, day by day, month by month —don't ever get out of the process where you are continually being filled with the Holy Spirit. Have you had

the second blessing? Sure, man, and the third, and the
fifth, and the hundredth, and the thousandth, and ten
thousandth; and I expect to get a whole bunch more. I've
got to keep on getting filled! Every day, every minute,
every time I sin.

Now what really happens is this: The first time a man
comes to the realization of what it means to commit
himself totally to Christ and to the Holy Spirit, it is usually so cataclysmic and wonderful that he makes it a
brand new thing and wants to get a new name for this
new experience. Usually the first time he is filled with the
Holy Spirit is so much greater than any other time and
greater than what he has had before in contrast with what
he has been as a carnal Christian that he calls it getting
the baptism. That's not getting the baptism—that is just
the first time he has been filled.

You may ask, "Why is a man filled with the Holy
Spirit?" The Holy Spirit never does anything without
purpose. He never does anything without a reason, and
the reason for the fulness of the Holy Spirit is clearly
stated. Jesus said in Acts 1:5, "John truly baptized with
water; but ye shall be baptized with the Holy Ghost not
many days hence." Sure enough, they were on Pentecost. "When they therefore were come together, they
asked of him, saying, Lord wilt thou at this time restore
the kingdom to Israel?" And he said that it isn't for you
to know. Don't worry about what is going to happen. He
said here is what I want you to worry about: "But ye shall

receive power, after that the Holy Ghost is come upon you: and ye shall be witnesses unto me both in Jerusalem, and in all Judaea, and in Samaria, and unto the uttermost part of the earth." Jesus said the purpose of being filled and baptized, immersed, annointed, introduced, or whatever you wish to call it, is to be a witness to Jesus Christ. And you cannot be one without it.

There was a purpose for which people had to speak in tongues in the New Testament. Remember on the day of Pentecost they all came together and Jesus wanted to let them be witnesses to the whole world, but the whole world could not understand them. They were there from every language under heaven and they spoke in one language and everyone heard in his own. There was a sensible reason—they had to hear it. Now, mark my word any time you have a King James version of the Bible which says unknown tongue, it is always in italics, indicating that it is not in the original Greek manuscript, and if it is not there it is erroneous. No Greek manuscript has the word "unknown" tongue in it. There is only one kind of tongue mentioned in the Bible—other tongues, other languages.

Further, if there is a bona fide experience, a personal edification in private for the believer, the new language of praise that exalts the Lord and strengthens him, it is a gift of God which comes unsought. There are schools of thought and even churches which advertise in the paper that they will teach you how to talk in tongues. It is ridiculous to think that you can teach anyone to speak in tongues. The Bible says that this is a gift of God. I know people who have the gift of making money. I have the gift of preaching and others, the gift of teaching. And, since tongues is a gift of God, it will be given as a private, personalized gift.

For me to go around and try to learn it is ridiculous! Once in awhile, when they were filled with the Holy Spirit, they did happen to speak, not in an unknown tongue, but in other tongues which could be understood by the person hearing. Also understand that sometimes they were filled with the Holy Spirit and walked on live coals. Sometimes they touched snakes and were not bitten. And sometimes they were filled with the Holy Spirit and gave all their money to the poor. Now, why doesn't everyone do *that* today? Let's don't make this thing the test of whether you've got it or not.

There are two problems with this "unknown tongue" business. One, is that it builds a bunch of Pharisees that go around condemning and judging everyone else and making the whole touchstone of theology, "Have you got it, brother?" It breeds superiority and pride. Pride is of the devil. And anyone who goes around asking: "Have you got it, have you got it?" is of the devil and out of hell! Secondly, it makes the Holy Spirit the most important corner of their doctrine and that is of the devil too. Mark my words—"When he comes," said Jesus, "he will not speak of himself. He will speak of me. He will exalt me." He is the darling of the Trinity and that doctrine which exalts the Holy Spirit is of the devil and not of the Holy Spirit.

That church, that teaching which exalts Jesus—that is of the Holy Spirit! I hope you are a Jesus denomination and not a Holy Ghost denomination and a Jesus preacher and a Jesus church. When you get off the track and start honoring the Holy Spirit, brother, you are off-base!

Do not be afraid that you are going to act foolish and do something weird, but simply commit yourself to Christ and be filled with the Holy Spirit.

You say, preacher, I'd really like to have a life of peace and a life where I did not get dragged down by sin so easily and I could handle my problems. Understand that the Bible never once promised to be an escape from problems. The Christian will probably have as many divorces and deaths, as many diseases, sicknesses, and as many heartbreaks as the nonbeliever. It says that in this world you are going to have tribulation. The Christian life is not an insurance policy against trouble, but security and inner-peace in the midst of trouble. If it weren't, people would become Christians for the wrong reasons. Remember this: Just as a diamond shows up most beautifully against the backdrop of black velvet, so does your Christian faith never have the diamond-like opportunity of sparkling to the world as much as it does against the backdrop of midnight and heartbreak.

You say: "Preacher, I would like to live in the world

of sickness, heartbreak, sin, and temptation and have inner composure and the fulness of the Holy Spirit. How do I become filled with the Holy Spirit?" I suggest the following:

1. The very fact that you have asked tells me that you are half way there. You have to want it. You must desire the fulness of the Holy Spirit more than anything else in the world. He says, "You will find me when you search for me with all of your heart."

2. You must repent of your sins. To repent means three things. It means to feel badly about your sin, acknowledge your sins to God, and then quit doing them. You must turn from your sin to God in total commitment.

3. Ask in faith believing. "Ask that your joy may be full." "Ask and you will receive." Ask in faith: "Dear Lord, right this moment, I want you to fill me with the Holy Spirit." Don't look for an emotion, for a language, for a new feeling. You receive in faith and believe in faith. Just the same as you receive Jesus in faith, you receive the Holy Spirit's fulness in faith, and only then are you filled with the Holy Spirit.

The worst thing you can do to a new convert when he has asked Jesus to come into his heart is to ask, "How do you feel?" It does not make any difference how he feels. The devil can deceive us about our emotions, but he cannot deceive us about the word of God. When you are doing eternal business with God, it is a divine transaction with the Lord. You receive the fulness of the Holy Spirit when you want him more than anything else in the world. He too fills you, not by feeling, but by faith.

The Holy Spirit is God, and your relationship to him is your relationship to God. Insult him—injure him—experience him—the decision is yours. Choose the former and you will die. Choose the latter—and live—live as you have never dreamed possible—controlled—filled by the life-giving power of the precious Holy Spirit.

V

**Why Doesn't God
Answer My Prayers?**

In Luke 1:5–13 we read: "There was in the days of Herod, the king of Judea, a certain priest named Zacharias, of the course of Abia: and his wife was of the daughters of Aaron, and her name was Elisabeth. And they were both righteous before God, walking in all the commandments and ordinances of the Lord blameless. And they had no child, because that Elisabeth was barren, and they both were now well stricken in years. And it came to pass, that while he [Zacharias] executed the priest's office before God in the order of his course, [or at the time for his group to do so] according to the custom of the priest's office, his lot was to burn incense when he went into the temple of the Lord. And the whole multitude of the people were praying without [outside] at the time of incense. And there appeared unto him an angel of the Lord standing on the right side of the altar of incense. And when Zacharias saw him, he was troubled, and fear fell upon him. But the angel said unto him, Fear not, Zacharias: for thy prayer is heard; and thy wife Elisabeth shall bear thee a son, and thou shalt call his name John."

As a descendant of Aaron, Zacharias was one of thousands of priests. There were too many priests, actually, and so it was not often that a man got to go in and perform the responsibilities of priest. This faithful man, Zacharias, looked forward to this day. Three times a year,

at the Feast of the Tabernacle, the Feast of the Passover
and the Feast of Pentecost. As his responsibility was the
burning of the incense, he was in the holy of holies.
There in the court of the priest as the people in the court
of the Israelites waited outside, the ceremony went
thusly: a whole burnt offering was given. It was a male
lamb without spot or blemish. It was given with an aura
of incense as though to wrap a sweet savor about it as
it was given to God on this occasion in behalf of all of
the people of all of Israel for the whole year through the
ministry of this man.

As he was praying in the Temple, the Bible tells us the
angel of the Lord spoke to him and said, "Thy prayer
is heard." Now you recall that for many decades he and
his wife had longed for a son, and yet there was no son
forthcoming. He was startled, he was afraid, he was unbelieving. He fell to his knees and did not believe his ears
nor his eyes. And yet the angel says clearly that after
these many years, "Thy prayer is heard." I confess to you
that though I have written a book which has sold many
copies on the subject of prayer, I feel very much uninformed on prayer. There is that about prayer which all
of us marvel at and about which many of us, all of us,
do not really understand very much. I think that here is
one of the most clear-cut truths about prayer in all of the
Bible. If there are three things we should understand
about prayer, they are all here in this one little story.
Again, I think they are the three most important truths

about prayer.

Number one: Delayed answers do not necessarily mean refusal.

Secondly: God is not very hard on us because we quit believing him.

And thirdly: The only reason for delayed answer is that God may give us a greater answer later on. Now we'll deal with these one at a time.

First of all, we find in the story the important truth that delay is not necessarily refusal. In fact the Christian should expect delay when he prays. Now to be sure, God will no more withhold from us those urgent, critical things that we must have right then, than we would withhold from our own child food and health and safety when he needs them. But God does oftentimes delay the answer to our prayers, and it is to be expected. But that delay does not necessarily mean refusal. In fact, you may be well assured that when it is prayed in faith, when it is in the will of God, when it is prayed in the name of Christ, and when we believe and it is offered from a consistent life, that *every prayer will be answered!*

Prayer that is delayed does not necessarily mean that it is a refusal but that the answer is on the way. And when a prayer is in the will of God, is raised from a consistent heart, and is prayed in faith and on the merits of the blood of Christ, it *will be answered! Always!* Maybe not today, maybe not tomorrow, but one day. Ultimately, we have the promise of God. I want us to notice some conditions under which God blessed this man although he did not answer his prayer then, but chose to delay the answer.

In the eighth verse "And it came to pass, that while he executed the priest's office . . ." he was being faithful to his responsibilities. As a member of the order of Aaron, he was a priest before God. But for year after year there had been no answer to his prayer. And yet he did not quit being a priest, he did not quit going to God's house, he did not quit bringing men to Christ, and that is the responsibility of a priest—to bring men to God. The Bible says that we are all kings and priests before God. I promise you that as the salt of the earth, as a witness with your life, with your money, with your faithfulness before your children—in every area of your life— that when you continue to execute the office of a Christian in fidelity and faithfulness to Christ, that God will see your faithfulness and without it you have no assurance of the answer to prayer but that with it, though he delay, *God will ultimately answer prayer.*

I have a friend in another city who is always calling me, always complaining because God doesn't bless him, God doesn't prosper him, God doesn't do things for him, God does not answer his prayers. My friend does not tithe, he is not a soul-winner, he does not read the Bible, he does not go to church. He wants, in fact, something for nothing. Well, it just doesn't work that way! God is a supernatural, prayer-power answering God, but there are some ground rules and some requirements laid down for the Christian. I'm not being legalistic at this point, but I want to be very honest and say that you don't need to flaunt it in God's face when your kids turn out bad, when you go bankrupt, when God doesn't answer your prayer, if you have not been serving the Lord. And that includes righteousness and purity of life, and holiness, and going to church, and giving God his tithe, and being a priest before God, and faithfully executing all that God requires. God is not just a kind of a spiritual granddaddy, who stands around passing out good things because he has nothing else to do. There are some requirements of faithfulness for the Christian.

When we are faithful to God and the answer still doesn't come, you may be assured that it is not a refusal, it is only a delay, which we shall see. Zacharias had prayed for years and it had never come, and yet he didn't quit God. He didn't quit being faithful to the Lord. He continued to execute the office of a priest. . . . Now notice another thing. The Bible says in the next verse "As his custom was," and in the rest of the verse "it was his lot to burn incense when he went in to the temple of the Lord. He not only served the Lord, he served the Lord in the Temple. Now it's one thing to be a Christian, it's another thing to be a Christian outside of faithfulness to the church. The clear-cut command of the Scripture is forsake not the assembling of yourselves together.

There's a fad these days which sounds good but it has

antiestablishment overtures, and many a sincere young person and many a dedicated Christian is totally misunderstanding how affected they are being by the attitude of the world against anything that is structured. I give an illustration: The song that's very popular called "Me and Jesus Got Our Own Thing Going." Now I like that, I really do. I think that's real cool—"Me and Jesus Got It All Together." Now they ought to stop right there, but they don't. They go on to say, "Man, we don't need no fancy choir, we don't need no fancy preachin', we don't need no fancy church, man, just me and Jesus, baby, got it all together." Well it doesn't work that way.

I remind you that the bride of Jesus Christ is the church. Jesus loved the church, Jesus died for the church. And Jesus has ordained the preaching of the gospel by the God-called ministry, the assembling of ourselves together in the New Testament Church through his Word. Now don't tell me, that you and Jesus got it all together and then knock the bride of the Lord Jesus Christ that he died for. It doesn't work that way. You and Jesus haven't got anything together, if you do not love his church and have his church together as a part of your life. God answered Zacharias' prayer, but it was while he was faithful to the office of God as a Christian, and while he was faithful in the temple of God.

Life can be a beautiful, wonderful Christian experience, but it will not be so if you make up your own rules. It will not be as you play God's ball game by your ground rules, but by his. There are requirements, and when they are met in consistency, then you may be assured that though he waits to answer your prayer, he is not necessarily refusing to answer it.

Number one: Delay does not mean refusal.

Number two: Though we are unfaithful, though we quit believing, God is really not very hard on us because we don't believe. Here's what I mean. When this man had prayed, he and his wife through the years, in their twenties and thirties and forties and fifties, I am sure that they believed God. But now they were past the time of life that it was possible, biologically and physically, for them to have children. They were aged and well-stricken in years; and perhaps at age eighty or ninety or maybe a hundred, God came to them and said, "Thy prayer is heard." Now what does Zacharias say? Did he say: "Oh that's good. I knew it was going to happen all the time." No not at all. He was petrified. He was so unbelieving and so afraid, he fell in unbelief. He put his hands on his spiritual hips and said: "I don't believe it. Why, we're too old." But you see, although he had quit believing, hear me, there was a time in his life when he did believe. And God was rewarding that earlier faithfulness. I'm glad God doesn't strike us off in our weak moments, aren't you? I'm glad when circumstances are against us, and we don't believe God, that God doesn't say OK, I'll never answer your prayer again. Paul says it like this: "Though we are faithless, yet praise God he abideth faithful. He cannot deny himself." And he says that if we believe with just the tiniest grain of a mustard seed, we can move mountains. I am so grateful that our God still comes to us in a moment when we have quit believing and does not give up on us when we have given up on him. I urge you to keep on believing and keep on praying.

The third and last word is this: The only reason God delays an answer to prayer that he is going to answer, is so that he can do us the greater good. There are things that God could do for us now which would be limited by not waiting so that he could do much more for us after awhile. They wanted that son when they were twenty, or thirty, or forty years old, but God did not give it to them until they were eighty, or ninety, or a hundred years old for the following reasons.

Historians agree that perhaps the reasons for the survival of the New Testament church, physically speaking, is the quality of converts with which the New Testament church began in its inception. And, these were converts under the ministry of John the Baptist. What kind of preaching produced that kind of convert? The Bible says that John the Baptist never saw a man, never set foot in civilization until he first started to preach "the kingdom is at hand." In other words, he had spent at least thirty years in the barren wilderness by himself, alone with God, getting ready for his ministry. I raise the question, where did a five-, or ten-, or fifteen-year-old boy get that kind of faith? that kind of religion? and that kind of stick-to-itivity? I'll tell you where he got it—he got it from his godly mother and dad who had been through the same thing. They had passed on to him, "Son, believe God in the desert just as you do on the blooming mountain." Had God given them their answer to their prayer as young husband and wife, their son would not have been able to receive the benefits of waiting which ultimately made him the kind of preacher that he was, and the New Testament forerunner of Jesus Christ.

While Zacharias was in the temple praying for the Messiah to come, it was right then, only by waiting until then, that God could let the Messiah come. He wanted the greater prayer answered. He wanted a son, yes. But, the Jews wanted the Messiah to come, and that was the main thing. But the Messiah could not come until the New Testament forerunner was ready to come just before him. Jesus had to come when all things were ready—in the fulness of time. Zoroastrianism had not yet gripped the world. That star was not yet ready to shine. The political and social system was not yet ready for the Messiah. Things were not at an all-time low. He could not come as a dry root out of the ground until things were precisely right. Nor could he come until his forerunner had come six months ahead of that time. If he had come at the time of his forerunner, things would have been for naught. God had to delay the answer to that prayer until everything was right so that he could give them a greater answer.

I hope you never forget that there is no greater truth than this, that our good God wants to get us to the ultimate ocean of his blessing. If it means a little side creek trickling down to the right and he says, "No, wait a little while here, the time is not yet," that he is only waiting and delaying so that he can give us what we really want.

Augustine in his *Confessions* writes how his mother longed more than anything else in the world for him to be a Christian, and she knew if he left her and went out into the world, he would never be saved. While he was sailing from Carthage to Rome, he lied to her and slipped off and said, "I am going abroad to see a friend." And, all the time she was up in the church praying to God not to let him go saying: "He'll never be saved if he goes to worldly Rome. I will never see him again." She left the church brokenhearted because God had not given her what she wanted. Later, he was saved, not in spite of going to Rome, but because he did go to Rome, for he had a date there with destiny. I promise you with all my heart, in the name of the unchanging word, that delayed answer, when we are in the will of God and praying in faith from a consistent life, does not mean refusal. Fortunately, God is not too hard on us for our loss of faith during the delay.

Thirdly and ultimately, the only reason for the delay is that our God might do something bigger and greater for us.

We all pray and tell God how to give us what we want. But we view the parade of life from ground level. God is standing on top of the hotel. He sees the beginning and the ending, as the whole thing goes by. He knows where it is going and how to fit it in. Whether or not we really trust him and really believe in his goodness and concern for us is the ultimate test of our faith. Believing when we can see where it is going is one thing. But believing when it looks like the answer is no is another. I urge your faith and trust, consistent and continuing, upon the ultimate goodness of our benevolent Lord.

VI
What Do I Do with My Sins?

I would like to deal with what we Christians need to have before we can be filled with the Holy Spirit, and that is a simple *A, B, C,* understanding of what we are to do with our sins when we, as Christians, sin. How do we handle the matter of daily sin? Let us look very closely at the words one-by-one in 1 John 1:9: "If we confess our sins, he is faithful and just to forgive us our sins, and to cleanse us from all unrighteousness."

If, the first word. Notice that the forgiveness of our sins is conditional, not automatic. We are talking about two different things—sin and sins. There is a difference. When a person is saved, his sin is dealt with. The principle of sin and the sins that he has committed because of that principle which is in him is forgiven. But, this sin principle has not been totally eradicated. One does not become perfect at salvation. He becomes forgiven. The Bible tells us that if we, then, we who are believers, confess our sins, he is faithful and just to forgive us of our sins and to cleanse us from all unrighteousness. It does not do an unsaved person any good to come to God and say: "Dear Lord, I want you to forgive me for cheating on my income tax or stealing cookies out of the cookie jar when I was a kid, or for getting drunk the last two Saturday nights." Those are sins—specifics, individual things which men do as a result of the fact that they are sinners. Think of it as a flower garden which

grows weeds or grows flowers. There is the thing which
produces the fruit. You can come along and pull up the
weeds or snip the flowers, but you are only dealing with
the symptom. You have to deal with the problem.

Unsaved man does not need to confess his individual
sins, that would take forever. All the unsaved man does
is deal with his sin, the principle of his nature, which is
set in opposition against God. So, the unsaved man acknowledges before God that he is a sinner, and the very
totality of his being is set against God. There is nothing
good in him. All have sinned. In the flesh dwelleth no
good things. All of man is set against God. We must ask
God to forgive that, erase that, take it out, cleanse that.
I acknowledge that a sinful nature is operative in me.
And, God forgives that sin.

But, when a man becomes a Christian, the principle
of sin, though forgiven, is not eradicated. It is still there.
There is still something in us which continues to sin.
And, because of that which has been forgiven, but not
removed else we would be perfect, we continue to com-
mit sins. It is correct to say that a Christian has been
saved. But it is also correct to say that he is being saved.
It is also correct to say that he will one day yet be saved.
You say, "I have never heard anything like that from a
Baptist preacher!" Let us examine it.

When I say, "I have been saved," of what am I speaking? I have been saved from the penalty of sin and am
not estranged from God. But I have an acknowledged,

forgiven nature that is in opposition against God. But also I now have a new nature. So there are two natures at work within me. I am forgiven for that first and the potential of victory over it is a reality in my life. I am not going to hell. I have been saved from the penalty of my sin. But the more I grow in grace, the more I learn to confess my sins, plural, keep them up to date, the more I become like Christ, the more I am controlled by the Holy Spirit, the more there is of him and less of me. I am daily being saved from the power of sin. A brand new convert doesn't realize his potential power over sin. He must grow and be saved daily from sin's power.

Then, one day, when a man is glorified and goes to heaven, he will be saved from the very presence of sin. Salvation means that there is a principle of rebellion within me. I acknowledge that and ask for a new nature. I ask God to come into my heart and engraft in me a brand new nature. And, this he does. The old nature is forgiven but not eradicated. Consequently, I now have two natures—the old and the new. They vie with each other for control of my life.

How many of you, since you have been saved, have never sinned one sin? Of course we have, so it is still there. Now as we are daily becoming more like Christ, the old nature is getting under control and the new nature is growing. The old nature is being held in check, and Christ is becoming real and full and in control in my life. But, this does not mean that I will never sin again because in any life—the meanest of sinners or the fairest of saints—you still find sin to be a problem. A person still commits sins which are the result of the old nature of sin, still present, still operative with which he must deal but for which he is no longer condemned or guilty. Now he has two natures and the old nature produces sins.

After one is saved, he no longer finds merit in confessing his sin. We do not need to keep coming to God and dealing with the matter of sin, for we insult him. We call him a liar when we doubt our salvation, when we doubt that he has saved us. Now we must deal, not with sin, but with sins.

Notice he says, "If we confess our sins," which is plural. So we must deal daily with our sins. We must stay in a constant state of fellowship.

Let's talk about two words—relationship and fellowship. Relationship is established at salvation when God deals with the nature of my sin, which I acknowledge and he forgives and makes me just in my relationship with him because I have acknowledged that principle of sin in me. But, now, because I have been born into the relationship of his family, I never again need to deal with the relationship. But I can get out of fellowship.

I have two sons, ages nine and ten. When they do something wrong, they do not come to me and say, "Daddy, I want to be your little boy again." They can only become my little boys once. The relationship is irrevocable and has been firmly established. When they do wrong, they need to acknowledge the specific thing they have done wrong to get back in fellowship. The Bible promises amazing things to the believer who stays in fellowship with God. The Bible says, "If we abide in him and his words abide in us, ye can ask whatever ye will and it shall be done unto you." What does it mean to abide in him? One thing: simply to remain in a state of constant unbroken fellowship. Abide in Christ so that there is never anything between us, that we may maintain a state of constant, unbroken fellowship. In that state of fellowship, everything is promised to the believer.

What breaks fellowship? Sins—specific things that we do. So we must learn to confess our sins, to keep them confessed up-to-date, and I might say that they are to be enumerated individually, confessed and acknowledged immediately. If you are driving down the road in perfect fellowship with God and a wrong thought comes to your mind, without taking your eyes off the road, you should ask God to forgive that wrong thought. You then are in that perfect fellowship again with him.

When a wrong thought, a desire, lust, hatred, or anything wrong comes to mind and you do not confess it immediately, the power line—the fellowship between you and God is short-circuited. So keep those sins confessed up-to-date.

The Campus Crusade people have a little slogan called "Spiritual Breathing." I really like it. They say there are

two parts in Spiritual Breathing. One is exhaling sin by
confession and the other is inhaling the fulness of the
Spirit. When any sin comes to your heart or mind, confess it, whether you are drying the dishes, swimming,
driving a car, or so forth. Exhale it, get it out. Then
inhale and say: "Lord, forgive me of that. Take away that
thought. Fill me again with the Holy Spirit that I have
driven into one corner of my heart because of this sin
that I have committed."

Let us look at this word "confess" for a moment. Right
after I started out as a young preacher many years ago,
the second revival I preached, I had the privilege of
preaching in a rather large church in Oklahoma City. Dr.
Robert Scales was the pastor of the Trinity Baptist
Church. The former pastor of that church was attending
and I was trying to preach on Sunday morning on prayer
and the confession of sins and he came up to me and
said, "Son, would you like to know what that word 'confess' really means?" He said, "You did fine, but you did
not go far enough."

To confess in this context means to agree with God
as to his opinion of, to be in agreement with God. It does
not simply mean to confess or to acknowledge. It means
to agree. It does not mean to come to God and acknowledge that you have done something. It means to change
your perspective, to turn all the way around, not only to
acknowledge and repent and quit doing it, but also to
change your mind about it. You must learn to keep your

sins immediately confessed up-to-date.

The last thought is this: The Bible tells us if we confess our sins, God is faithful and just to forgive us our sins and to cleanse us by his blood of all unrighteousness. Some people have guilt complexes from which they can get no release because they do not believe that God has forgiven them. The memory of things done, even though confessed, continues to torment and destroy them. The Bible most assuredly says that a sin thusly acknowledged, confessed, and repented of is forgiven. Let me say to you that what God forgives, God forgets. He puts them behind his back as far as the East is from the West and remembereth them against us no more.

There are many things about the nature of God that I do not understand but that I accept. One of them is his perfect capacity to remember and his perfect capacity to forget. If you were to speak to God and God were to talk back verbally to you in conversation about a confessed sin over which you were having trouble, you will find the conversation going something like this: "Dear Lord." "Yes." "Do you remember that sin that I confessed to you last week?" "No, I don't. What sin?" You see, God has forgotten it. And you insult God and destroy yourself when you perpetually come to God with the same sin over and over and over. You must take God at his word. He does what he says. Many people in sincerity call on God to save them and go to their grave with a troubled, unsettled, and unsure mind about their salva-

tion. I ask people who are having serious doubts about
their salvation, "Have you really asked God in faith to
save you and meant it?" "Oh, yes, I have done that
hundreds of times." "No wonder you are troubled. No
wonder you are confused. No wonder your spiritual relationship with God is a mess." God does not do what he
does on the basis of how you feel or how you logically
reason it to be, but on what he says in his word. God and
his word are synonymous. God's word will not change.
All that he does for man he does on the basis of our
willingness to believe his word. There is nothing for you
he will do—there is nothing that he can give you except
in response on the basis of your believing his word. He
says, "If you confess, I am faithful and just to forgive."

If you are one who still has doubts and cannot forget
your past sins, let me suggest a tiny physical help for you
by visualizing your faith. Get a pen and paper and write
out that sin for the last time. Go to the sink and take a
match and burn it. You say, "Dear Lord, as the fire is
consuming this paper, just so, I am believing for the last
time the blood of Jesus to consume, burn, and destroy
my sin—that sin for which I still feel guilty. I am claiming
your word in 1 John 1:9, believing that you have cleansed
me. I will never insult you and your word by bringing
it up again. I am through with it." Then, go your way.
As other sins come, as other sins shall, immediately keep
that fellowship together by acknowledging and confessing, naming those individual sins, claiming the cleansing

of the blood in faith and going right on in a state of unbroken fellowship, for in that state, God promises everything for the believer.

"If we confess our sins, he is faithful and just to forgive us our sins, and to cleanse us from all unrighteousness" (1 John 1:9).

VII

**What Does God
Expect from Me?**

John the Baptist, it is said, is recorded of Jesus as being the greatest man ever born of woman. To me that is wonderful, but somehow it is not quite as warm, it is a bit more categorical and historical than what our Lord said of David.

The Bible says of David that he was a man after God's own heart. Between the two expressions, I find that of David to be more meaningful and personal. David was a man after God's own heart! That is to say that there are some things people misjudge about what is important to God, that David had in his heart. As a young man of thirty years of age, he was crowned king of his people. When he came home, thousands of people would line the streets to pay homage to him. He was probably the most brilliant, the most handsome, the most popular of all the kings of the Jews. Here was a man that was my kind of man. God said, "Here is a man after my own heart."

Contrast that with the physical record of David. When he was a young man, he rose perhaps too quickly to the height and position of responsibility that was his. He was drinking the heavy wine of success and he forgot his spiritual life. It was customary for Jewish people to pray morning, afternoon, and night but David thought that he could go it alone, so he missed his noonday prayer meeting. The Bible says that as he was walking on the rooftop at noon, he looked down and lusted over Bath-sheba. It was not an accident. It was a planned thing when he connived to bring her to his palace, to kill her husband, to commit adultery with her, and to lie about the whole thing. Lying, adultery, and murder—the three worst things that can be said about a man. But here we have the ironic situation in the life simultaneously of one individual that while he committed the greatest sins a man can commit, yet God said of this same man, "Here is a man after my own heart."

Obviously, men have some wrong standards. Jesus said that men often appear righteous and may not commit the physical act of lying, murder, jealousy, hatred, or lust, in their heart they are violent, filthy, mean, and lustful. And, the man who may commit an act on the outside and be greatly remorseful and sorrowfully repent is far greater in God's eye than a man who in his own proud, self-sufficiency, thinks about what he did not do but wishes he could do. So, God goes far beyond the act to the intent. The entire crux of the Sermon on the Mount, in my opinion, is that the legalistic system of laws by which the Jews judged and controlled everything that they did was not nearly as important to our Lord as the motive, the character, the instinct within a man that caused him to do what he did and did not do. God goes far beyond rules and law to intent, character, and loyalty of the heart.

There is no doubt that David was a great sinner. But,

David was a great repenter as well. What then does God
see in a person that he requires and respects? In Psalm
51 we find David's psalm of repentance. In my mind,
verses 10–11 say so well what God looks for in man and
what David did not want to lose. "Create in me a clean
heart, O God; and renew a right spirit within me. Cast
me not away from thy presence; and take not thy holy
spirit from me." In this passage of Scripture David opens
up to us that which he understands to be the most important thing in the world about a man, and that which is
of importance to God who made such a statement—the
spirit of a man. I don't care whether a man has been to
seminary and has a hundred doctor's degrees. If he does
not have the right kind of spirit, he is not going to be
a great preacher. It doesn't matter how successful a person may be or how rich or affluent. If he doesn't have
the right spirit, he is not going to be a great person.

The spirit of a man, the right kind of spirit, has true
honor and true humility and charity. How many times
have you been around people who did not particularly
impress you the first time you met them? But the more
you got to know them, the more you were around them
you knew there was something warm about them, something you liked very much. Something about them which
you could identify with, made you want to be near
them—you just enjoyed this person. You enjoyed their
spirit. The spirit of a man is what makes the man.

In Psalm 51 he is understanding and explaining for us

that there is much more than just a fleshly spirit, the spirit of a good, warm personality that makes a man. The thing that made his spirit different was the Holy Spirit in him which tempered his spirit and made it the kind of spirit that it was. A man not possessed by the Holy Spirit is a man incomplete in his mind, a man not dependable, a man with more kinds of problems than you can imagine. But, when all of the powers of the mind and heart and being are brought into subjection and control by the presence of the Holy Spirit in his life, the Spirit of God is the oil in the moving part of the motor of life, and makes it all hum and purr like a new car instead of rattling like a clanker. So, David, more than anything, wanted this renewed power from the Holy Spirit.

What does the Holy Spirit do in men which gives them a spirit that is special? He produces love—for God is love. That does not mean God is an abstraction, but it means more than anything else, the totality of God's personality is love. When men are filled with God, they love. You cannot love your husband, wife, children, or pastor, or employer unless there is love in you. The spirit of the Holy Spirit in us makes us people who love. To genuinely love other people is the single important quality and trait about a man in the mind of God. God wants people who really love each other, for in so doing, we redemonstrate the life of God. We re-create God because God is love and love is a godly relationship. And that is what he expects of us. Men cannot live without

God and men who have God cannot help but love. Above everything, God is love. And, when we are filled with God, we have true love.

I would like to suggest three examples of an unordinary, superspiritual quality of love, which could only come from God, demonstrated in the life of David.

First, David loved the truth. He did not care who it hurt or how much it cost as long as the truth was done. You remember that David, after he had committed his great sin, was confronted by a faithful preacher, named Nathan, the prophet. A preacher who does not confront you with your own sin in love for your own good and tell you the truth is like a doctor who knows you have cancer but gives you something for the "itch." He is not your friend. He is your bitterest enemy. So, Nathan, the prophet, the great preacher came to David and told him about a terrible sin that had been committed and in the description he described David's sin. He wanted David's opinion before he made it personal. David, hearing of what had been done by someone who had everything who broke up a home of someone who had very little, said, "That man shall repay fourfold." That was the truth, but the truth against himself. Nathan said, "David, thou art the man." If it had been Mary, Queen of Scots, she would have abrogated the law. Louis the Fourteenth would have declared himself above the law. But what did David do? David did not change the law. He did not as Victoria would have done, simply dismiss the poor crea-

ture and hire another court preacher, even though it hurt
him, destroyed him, even though it was the truth against
him, it was the truth, and the truth of God must be
honest. David said, "I have sinned against God." The
truth crushed him, but it was the truth and David loved
the truth.

It is amazing the way people react in situations when
the truth is at stake, when it confronts them. It would
have been so easy to have fired the preacher, changed
the law, lied about it, one of a hundred defense mech-
anisms by which one would protect himself. But the word
of God, God's moral law which had been broken, even
though he had broken it, was at that moment far more
important to David than the fact that it had destroyed
him. He said: "You are right. I am guilty. God forgive
me. I have sinned." David loved the truth that all men
are created equal. It may be the truth which disturbs
them. But, if it is the truth, it is truth. To love the truth
regardless of how much it hurts you or how it affects you
personally and to stand by the truth and to defend the
truth and support the truth at any personal sacrifice—
this is what makes the man a great man. David loved the
truth.

Secondly, I would suggest to you that David loved his
friends. Someone has said you better be careful how you
treat people on the way up, for you will meet them again
on the way back down.

When David rose to the top, he did not forget those

whom he loved. You will remember that his bitterest enemy was King Saul. Three times Saul tried to kill David. Thrice David's life was in jeopardy. Yet Saul had a son whose name was Jonathan, and Jonathan was David's best friend. David loved Jonathan dearly and the fact that Jonathan's father was trying to kill him made no difference to David.

Many years after Saul and Jonathan had died, David, in his old age, began to think about his revered friendship with his now deceased, loving, lifelong friend, Jonathan. "I wonder if there is anyone in this world who is a descendant of Jonathan. I wonder if he has any living relatives, that I might find him and do something good for him in memory of my good friend, Jonathan."

David searched until he found a boy named Mephibosheth. He was a cripple and could not walk or stand on either of his legs. David restored his part of the kingdom to the son of Jonathan, who was the rightful owner. "Bring the boy home. Let him sit at my table. Let him wear my clothes, come to my house. I will assume all responsibility for him until his death because he is Jonathan's son, and Jonathan was my friend."

It seems that God saw something in the heart of this man that made him think, "There is my kind of man. There is a man after my own heart, a man with true character, a man at all times, not just idly waiting for the opportunity to come, but who eagerly and aggressively assaults the problem and is friendly to people, the kind

of people that Jesus loved. David loved the truth. And
he had an unusual love for his friends that was definitely
the result of spiritual love for God.

The last word is this: David loved regardless. Physically speaking, the most important possession to David
was his kingship. He was the most successful and popular
of all the Jewish kings. In fact, the throne to which the
Messiah will come has been respected and honored
through the years and has come to be known as the
throne of David. This is symbolic of the rule of the Jewish
people, for they want their era of peace to be like it was
when David was on the throne. David was a great king.

One day someone tried to take away that which was
most important to him, his kingdom. That someone was
his son, Absalom. The kingdom began to fall. His daugh-
ter, Tamar, was attacked. His kingdom fell, his baby
died. When you plant the wild seeds, they start coming
up fast. As the soldiers of David's army rose to meet
Absalom's men one night in an attack, they filled Absalom's body with poison darts. When they brought the
news of his death to David, he did not say: "Great, I have
my kingdom back. I'm glad that rascal is dead." No.
Listen to the agony which filled David's heart as he
prayed: "Absalom, Absalom, oh my son, Absalom, would
to God I had died in thy stead." It didn't matter that
Absalom had tried to kill him, to destroy his kingdom
and take away everything that he had—Absalom was his
boy, he loved him with a love that is only possible by the

re-creative work of the Holy Spirit, creating love in us, the kind of love that is like God's love.

I suppose fifty times a year someone writes me a letter asking me to find their son in Houston whom they believe to be living in a hippy colony. I would say that we have been successful about a third of the time.

So many times, these parents ask, "Has my boy cut his hair, cleaned up, taken a bath? He's not coming back in my house until he dresses and looks like us and apologizes." I don't blame those kids if they don't go back. You see, true love is not vindictive. Love loves regardless. This is not "soap opera" love, nor is it magazine love. This is miraculous love like the heart of God has regardless of anything and can only be in you when God is in you. Only the Holy Spirit in you can make you that kind of an unusual, loving person. That is what makes a man a man after God's own heart. That is what God sees that is important to him. No greater compliment was ever paid to man, no grander goal was ever set for men than that would be said of us, filled by the loving holy power of the Holy Spirit, that we should be men and women after God's own heart. For this is what is important to him—this is what he expects of us.

VIII

Tell Me the Truth
About Demon Possession

When Lucifer was banished from heaven it appears that a third of the angels sided with him and were banished as well. Because they still hate God and cannot get back at God, they come to the second highest of God's creations, the earth and continue the rebellion against Jesus Christ through his beloved creatures, human beings. Here on this earth Lucifer transforms himself into Satan, and the fallen angels become demons. Demons cannot be everywhere at once. They are not omnipresent; they are not omnipotent. They cannot be everywhere at once. They can do some things but they cannot do everything. Jesus Christ in the power of the Holy Spirit is everywhere at once. But it is not possible for the devil to be everywhere; it is not possible for demons to be everywhere. Demons cannot reproduce because they are fallen angels and angels are sexless beings. But there were seemingly enough to begin with to have at least one for everybody that lived or ever will live on this earth. Some have been inhabited by two thousand demons.

Now there is a lot of hairline theology to split here but it really doesn't matter. I don't believe that it is possible for a Christian to be demon possessed, that is to say completely controlled. The Holy Spirit who never leaves us will never permit 100 percent control by demons in our lives. It is possible for a Christian to be demon influenced, to be demon powered and demon lead astray, but never to be totally given over to the complete 100 percent control of demons.

In the last days God is going to pour out his Spirit on all flesh. When God pours out his spirit on all flesh, one thing happens. Men are filled with an intense appetite for God. An intense spiritual hunger is created. That is what is happening today. A revival is taking place. But an ironic situation occurs. While men are hungering for God, men uninformed about the gospel do not know they are hungering for God. They only know they are hungering; they only know they are upset; they only know they are longing. There are mixtures of emotions and frustrations and unfulfilled needs vying for fulfilment inside of them. They are confused and bewildered and frustrated. And when the church does not take advantage at any cost of every opportunity to rush into that vacuum and tell them about Jesus Christ, men turn to false spiritual experiences, and pseudoreligions, and pseudospiritual experiences occur. That is precisely what is happening in our society today in the occult.

Satan is an arch counterfeiter. There is a satanic trinity. There is a satanic church, a false plan of salvation, false scripture, false eschatological outline. Everything that Jesus has, Satan has counterfeited. They are all pseudoimitations of the real thing. The Bible tells us that because this is happening—demonology and the spread of demons and the spread of men hungering and searching for real spiritual experiences and not being informed they are to be found in Jesus Christ—will in the last days give heed to old wives' fables and turn to a hundred false spiritual kinds of experiences. And today demonology and witchcraft and Satan worship and spiritism and spiritualism are abounding in our country, all over the world for that matter. Cyril Black, outstanding leader of Parliament has said that 80 percent of the people of England at one time or another experience Satan worship. And he further adds that there are more people practicing witchcraft and attending Satan churches than all of the Christian churches combined in the British Isles. In 1965 *McCall's* magazine found that only 10 percent of all Americans believe in the devil. Today, seven years later, 65 percent of all Americans believe in a literal, personal devil, and well that they should.

The Bible says the devil is a person. He is not a spirit, not just an influence, he is real. He walks and talks, the Bible says he lives and breathes, he quotes Scripture. He was cast out of heaven, resisted by Jesus and the disciples. You say, preacher, where is it going to end? The Bible says it is going to end in hell. God created hell for the devil and his angels. Those who chose to follow him in this life, rather than following Christ are simply allowed to follow him right into hell in the next life. That is where the devil and his fallen angels are going to go, and that is where it is going to end.

The television talk shows have recently had someone on who was a practicing witch. Recently in New York City a store opened for the sale of articles to be used in the practice of witchcraft. I am not joking. You can buy a bottle of dried bat's blood or the latest style of genuine wolf fangs in New York City. We have Satan worshipers in Houston, in San Francisco, and all around the country.

What are the signs that an individual is possessed by the devil? How can I know that I am being influenced by a spirit inside of me that is crying out that is in reality a satanic spirit. How can I know that someone else is? There are many signs and I could in no way, shape or form cover all of them in this chapter. Of course, ultimately it is not possible for an evil spirit to acknowledge that Jesus Christ has come into the flesh, that he is the Son of God incarnate in human flesh. There are some very respectable Protestant denominations that deny that Jesus Christ is God come in the flesh and some that are not so respectable that shall remain unnamed.

In Mark 5:1–19 we read the story of a man who was demon possessed. Understand that there are other indications. We shall look briefly at just five of them. Five marks of a man controlled by demons. "And they came over unto the other side of the sea, into the country of the Gadarenes. And when he was come out of the ship, immediately there met him out of the tombs a man with an unclean spirit, who had his dwelling among the tombs; and no man could bind him." Now let's get a picture of this man who was demon possessed. He was possessed of an unclean spirit. Nobody could bind him, not even with chains.

> "Because that he had been often bound with fet-
> ters and chains, and the chains had been plucked
> asunder by him, and the fetters broken in pieces:
> neither could any man tame him. And always, night
> and day, he was in the mountains, and in the tombs,
> crying, and cutting himself with stones. But when he
> saw Jesus afar off, he ran and worshipped him, and
> cried with a loud voice, and said, What have I to do
> with thee, Jesus, thou Son of the most high God?
> I adjure thee by God, that thou torment me not."

Now this is the demon inside of him talking. "For he said unto him, Come out of the man, thou unclean spirit. And he asked him, What is thy name? And he answered, saying, My name is Legion: for we are many." There were many demons in him. Not just one.

> "And he besought him much that he would not
> send them away out of the country. Now there was
> there nigh unto the mountains a great herd of swine
> feeding. And all the devils besought him, saying,
> Send us into the swine, that we may enter into them.
> And forthwith Jesus gave them leave. And the un-
> clean spirits went out, and entered into the swine;
> and the herd ran violently down a steep place into
> the sea, (they were about two thousand;) and were

choked in the sea. And they that fed the swine fled, and told it in the city, and in the country. And they went out to see what it was that was done. And they come to Jesus, and see him that was possessed with the devil, and had the legion, sitting, and clothed, and in his right mind: and they were afraid. And they that saw it told them how it befell to him that was possessed with the devil, and also concerning the swine. And they began to pray him to depart out of their coasts. And when he was come into the ship, he that had been possessed with the devil prayed him that he might be with him. Howbeit Jesus suffered him not, but saith unto him, Go home to thy friends, and tell them how great things the Lord hath done for thee, and hath had compassion on thee."

Five things about the man who was demon possessed.
1. He was unclean. He was dirty. There are some signs that things are Christian and signs that they are not. There are characteristics of righteousness and characteristics of devilment. And one of the main signs of Christianity is that a man who is to be like Jesus Christ is to be clean. Everything about the devil is dirty. The Bible again and again speaks about the purity and the whiteness and the holiness and the cleanness and the righteousness of the robe and the garment of white that the Christian has.

One of the main signs that a man is controlled by the devil is that he has an obsession for dirtiness. He likes to be where it is unclean. Now a Christian may fall into the pigpen, but he doesn't like it, because that is not his nature and he will want to get clean again. But the unsaved man falls into the mud pen of sex or drunkenness or filth or dirty stories or whatever and likes to stay there. He likes the nightclubs, he likes to booze it up, he likes to gamble, he likes to run around with women, he likes to live like the devil, he likes to tell dirty stories, he is just unclean. That is his nature. There are a lot of people who come to church every Sunday morning who are fooling themselves into thinking they are saved when in reality they are as lost as a goose in a hailstorm because in reality, in secret, in privacy they are unclean and possessed with unclean spirits.

In America we do not allow open cesspools. I have been in South America in Guyana, for example, where open cesspools run right down the sides of the sidewalks. But there are plenty of moral cesspools within ten blocks of our church that are filthy and ought to be shut down. Many Christians like to frequent those places. When you are around in your office and you hear people telling dirty stories, are you offended? Are you embarrassed? Do you leave or do you like to tell your nasty story? Do you really enjoy feeding on filth? One of the signs of demon possession is that the demonic spirit likes that which is unclean.

2. The unclean man likes to abide where there is death. The Bible says he dwells among the dead. He likes to hang out in the graveyards. He doesn't like to go to church, he doesn't enjoy Sunday School. He would rather go to the graveyard. The Bible says in the book of Psalms we are the living among the dead. Not by our actions, but by our habitat. We must live among the spiritually dead in the world. But to live among them, to be a witness to them, to love them, to be a redeeming factor in society is one thing, but to enjoy it and to make it our habitat and to live in that kind of life and stay there is a different thing. This man enjoyed being around death. His nature was to be around unspiritual people. Some folks had rather hear a sermon about death than hear a sermon about tithing, and to hear about witnessing, to be with Christian people and to love the things of God and sing praise to him. They had much rather go to a rock concert than to hear "Amazing Grace" on Sunday morning. They are just much more at home with the spiritually dead than with the spiritually alive.

3. A demon-possed man is a violent man. He has a mean spirit. He is antagonistic, he is critical, he is gripey, he is negative, he is belligerent, he is a troublemaker, he is caustic. He has a mean, violent spirit. Somebody told me about a Bible class they had at one church for the mavericks, for those who were always kicking up a fuss. This man always liked to be in a fuss. He didn't like it where it was cool and quiet. He didn't like normality. He

didn't like calm, collective reasoning. He was hankering for a fight.

A famous preacher once said that if you are going to get ahead in the world, you have got to be against some things. "Get against something," he said, "get in a fight." I don't believe that at all. I remember our Lord saying something about when the devil comes in like a flood, don't get an axe or a gun, raise up the standard against him. The standard is the cross. We're not fighters, we're cross-lifters. One policeman said to me not too long ago, "I have not seen crowds as violent as they are today." People are just naturally, basically mean. You pull up to a stop sign and you might take a couple of inches of somebody's space and they will look at you as if they could kill you. The world can so easily get triggered off with anger and meanness and short-temperedness.

I am committed to a ministry to black persons. We happily have them in our church. But, let me tell you something. The black people for many years have hungered for integration. You know what they want now? Separation. Black identity. I say to you that they don't know what they want. White people are the very same way. A group of white young people in a crowd in California beat up on a young man who was just walking down the street, when a policeman asked them why they did it, they said, "We just wanted to get somebody." I don't care if you are black or white or red or yellow, the

answer to what you are looking for is not to beat up on
somebody or to be integrated or separated, to be in a
gang or out of a gang or to be red or yellow or white
or anything else. It is to know Christ.

That violent, mean streak that is in people who make
up society is nothing but the devil. You can pass laws and
change schools until you are blue in the face, but you will
never have a well-ordered disciplined society until people have a settled, cool spirit inside of them that is the
spirit of love that Jesus Christ produces. The violence
of our society is a reflection of violence in human hearts.
A violent running here, flying there, excited maniac type
of existence, such as the demoniac exhibited and which
is in the lives of many, is nothing but a hunger for God
and spiritual need for the love of Jesus Christ.

4. This man had an overt desire for nakedness. The
Bible says they chained him and he came out of his
chains. If they put him in a house, he kicked the doors
down. If they put him in jail, he broke down the walls.
If they put clothes on him, he would tear them off. They
were always trying to reform him. Put him in a new
house, paint the house, get him a new job, he would quit
the job and kick the walls down. It didn't do him any
good. Something was wrong on the inside. He always
wanted to get free of everything. Verse 15 tells us that
when they came to the man they were amazed. He was
seated, he was quiet, he was clothed and in his right
mind. When he met Jesus Christ, he didn't have the

desire to tear his clothes off. He had a desire to put his clothes on.

When Jesus Christ comes into your life it gives you the tendency toward modesty. I wonder how far Christian women are going to go. I think you ought to look nice. I think you should dress according to the standard of what is accepted. I don't think you ought to have to go around with your dress down to your ankles. If it is an inch or two or three or four above your knees that is one thing. But when it gets half way up to your neck, that's another. Where are Christian women going to stop? There comes a point at which our Christian decency and our commitment to the Word of God may conflict with the standard of accepted social behavior. And there Christ and his Word have to rule. You don't always have to be like everybody else. In the Garden of Eden they didn't even know they didn't have their clothes on. But as soon as they sinned, God came to them and put some clothes on them.

When a man is not right with God, he just knows that there is a turmoil and a conflict and something wrong on the inside. There is something inside of him crying to get out. The spirit that is longing for God can't stand containment. He'll change his clothes, he'll change his habits, he'll change his home, he'll change his job, he will break off everything that is containing him, trying desperately for something he does not have and going nowhere looking for what he does not understand. In a society with conflicting laws and confusion, confused people and leaders that are as confused as those they are trying to lead, it is the responsibility of the church and its membership to keep its commitment to the evangelism of the city and let society and the world know that what they need is to be found deep down inside Jesus Christ. No law, no school, no government, no politician, no party is going to help us one single bit until we get down to the issues of the human heart and men are evangelized and won to Christ and the spirit of man is converted.

5. This man was characterized by the fact that he was controlled by another spirit, not his own. Jesus never spoke one word to the man. It wouldn't do any good. The man did not have the ability to speak for himself. He had lost that ability, he had given it over to the devil. Paul says in Romans, chapter 6 that we are to be careful to whom we yield ourselves servants, for then those we yield ourselves to, whether a servant of Christ ending in righteousness or of sin ending in death, that servant relationship will turn on us, and it will become our master. You see, Mother and Dad, when you do not bring your children to Sunday School, when they are not in church, you are almost turning them right over to the devil. You are robbing them of the only spiritual counter power which can defeat the control of the devil in the lives of your kids. You are just asking for it, you are just begging for it, you are sending them into a sick society,

into sick schools with students and teachers and princi-
pals and forces and influences that are just like we are.
No better, no worse. Just a common society, that is not
going to be instilling any basic spiritual principles in
their lives.

For society as a whole does not recognize the basic
nature of spiritual problems. By the time your kids are
in the fourth, fifth, sixth grades, unless you have them
in a Bible-preaching Sunday School and church you can
just about cross 90 percent of them off to the devil. You
might as well face it. We live in enemy territory. Demons
are coming in like flies, and many of you who have
wasted your chances with your kids and didn't bring
them to Sunday School, you didn't tithe, you didn't go
to prayer meeting, you didn't bring them to church, you
bring them to the preacher when they are fifteen, bewildered as to why you can't control them. What went
wrong? I have heard it a hundred times. "Preacher, I just
can't control him." And the truth of the matter is, you
really can't control him. And he can't control himself.
Many a man that is bound up in alcoholism, and dope,
and lust, and making money, and pleasure seeking, is
demon controlled.

Notice Jesus didn't even talk to the man. He talked to
the demon that was inside of him, and the demon talked
back. He couldn't talk to the man. The man couldn't
control himself. He had to deal with the demon that
controlled him. Charles Manson said time and time again

that he was aware of some mysterious power that came over him, a power which he could not control, which forced him to do things. And he was telling the truth. It is so awesome, it is so dangerous to live in our society and not to have Jesus. You say, "Preacher, is there no answer?" Jesus said that in this world though you do live in enemy territory, greater is he that is in you than he that is in the world! There is hope! There is power! The disciples would not even try to resist the devil themselves. The disciples said, "The Lord rebuke you." When the devil comes knocking on your door, you can't handle him. You have got to say, "There he is Jesus, go get him!" Jesus has got to do it and that is the truth.

Unless you are living a life filled and controlled by the Holy Spirit and you have got Jesus really down inside of you, let me tell you what will happen. You come down, you join the church, you adhere to set up principles. You get religion without getting saved, you get church membership without getting Jesus. You become an Episcopalian, a Methodist, or a Baptist without becoming a born-again Christian, you know what happens? All you get is a good dose of reformation and turning over a new leaf. You will cast out one demon, but the Bible says that man who casts a devil out of himself and doesn't let the spirit of God come in and let Jesus save him and control him is a sitting duck for seven other devils to come in. Reformation is worse than nothing at all.

I notice also that there are three prayers that are

prayed in this story. Two of them Jesus answered and
one he didn't. For one thing, the demons said, "Jesus
if you are going to cast us out, turn us into those swine."
Those demons knew it was better to inhabit a pig, than
to inhabit the pit. They knew what hell was like. They
didn't want to go there. They said send us to the swine,
don't send us to the pit. The Bible says that is exactly
what Jesus did. There were two thousand of them the
Bible says. They all ran violently out of their minds into
the sea and were drowned. That means that there had
to be one demon in each pig, that's two thousand. Mary
Magdalene was possessed of seven, but here was a man
that was possessed of two thousand. It can get that bad.
Out of your mind. Controlled by other powers. He answered that prayer and turned them into swine instead
of sending them back to hell. There was another prayer.
I like this one! When the demoniac was saved he wanted
to go into full-time evangelism. He got into the boat and
told Jesus, "I want to go wherever you go." Jesus said,
"No, friend, get off the boat. I want you to go back to
your home town where everybody knows you. Go back
to your neighborhood. Go back to your friends. Go back
to the office."

There was a third prayer. The fellows that owned the
swine saw what had happened. They lost their swine.
They didn't want Jesus around any more. They didn't
care that a couple of boys got saved. They didn't care
about revival coming and righteousness. All they cared

about was the bill. All they cared about was that it was costing them money. They said get out of town. We don't want any salvation. We don't want any revival. All these demons being cast out, are destroying our profits. No more pigs! We don't care if this man is saved or not. We have got to keep that bread in the bank! You know—I think they were demon possessed too. There is no value in this world that you can place on the ministry of Jesus Christ and on what he can do in our lives. And so Jesus answered their prayer. He departed out of their coasts. But he never came back again. He left them.

I believe that a church, a city, a man has in his life an increasingly fewer number of opportunities for salvation and for revival and for witness under the leadership of God. Some of you will make that decision and it will be the wrong one. You will decide not to tithe, not to join the church, not to rededicate your life, not to admit to God that there is a demon in your life that is greater than you that you can't control. If you turn away you may find that Jesus will never pass this way again. The most amazing thing in the world to me is the power that is in Jesus Christ to cast out demons, to defeat problems, to give victory in impossible situations.

IX

What's Happening to Our World?

The prophet Joel said, "In the last days I will pour out my spirit upon all flesh." But Paul said to Timothy: "This know also, that in the last days perilous times shall come. For men shall be lovers of their own selves, covetous, boasters, proud, blasphemers, disobedient to parents, unthankful, unholy, without natural affection . . ." and on and on the sordid account of society goes. When you read both of these, it seems that somebody has made a mistake. They cannot both be right. In the last days God's Holy Spirit will be poured out on all flesh. There will be a mighty turning to Christ and a worldwide revival.

Then you turn to 2 Timothy and you find that in the last days there will be a mighty decay of society. Men by the millions will turn to sin and there will be more filth, pornography, debauchery, immorality, disease, and corruption than the world has ever imagined. Two opposites—which is true? Well, the truth of the matter is that both of them are true. In fact, we have the ironic situation that just before the end of the world and the coming of Jesus Christ, both of these situations are going to arise in a parallel manner. And, in fact, one of them is going to serve as the catalyst to trigger off the other one. Here is how it is going to happen.

You and I as well informed Christians and church members need to understand what is going on in our

world. And it is only a symptom of what is being acted
out behind the scenes of society. The world is a stage
upon which a battle is being fought for one thing—for
the ultimate control of the world. Theologians and
politicians and psychologists and reformers and college
students and educators and sociologists can never understand society until they understand it against the
backdrop and framework of what is really happening,
what our God is about in this world.

You, of course, remember that before life began on
this earth as we understand it now our heavenly Father
presided over an angelic society in heaven. It seems that
there was Gabriel, the soft-spoken angel, the counterpart
of the Holy Spirit, if you please; and Michael, the counterpart of the Father, the angel of judgment; and Lucifer,
the counterpart of Jesus.

Lucifer in heaven was the most intelligent and powerful and beautiful of all created beings. And Jesus is the
most intelligent, the most powerful, the most beautiful
of noncreated beings. He was not created. He is eternal.
It seems from the book of Isaiah that after centuries of
being willing to be subservient to Christ one day Lucifer
was no longer happy to be second in command. One day
his heart was filled with pride. After years of being willing to say, "Thy will be done," one day he said the first
two words back to back that introduced sin. When
Lucifer said, "I will," sin began. Listen, "I will rise above
God." "I will exalt myself above the throne of God." "I

will be like the most high." "I will—I will."

I have a Christian psychologist in my church. One day he said to me: "Preacher, do you want to know what sin is? The psychological definition of sin?" I said, "Tell me." He said, "Sin, psychologically, is an attitude that wishes God were dead." Sin is an attitude which wishes that any restraint and control and authority and government and discipline which is but a symbol of control of God over man in life did not exist. It wants to do its own thing. It wants to create a life-style totally devoid of control, in which man is god and he does whatever he gets good and ready to do. And that one simple proposition is indeed what sin is. In short, one day Lucifer declared war on God for the control of the world and the control of the universe.

Lucifer said we are going to create a life-style in this world, in this universe of lawlessness. Without law, without control, without restraint, without discipline, where every man is free to do as he pleases. That was Satan's original proposition. And it is one from which he has not deviated. Now when Satan, Lucifer, declared war on Jesus, Jesus could have crushed him and destroyed him then and there. He did not. He waited; he put it off and he banished him from heaven because nothing sinful and unholy can stay in the presence of a holy God. So where did he go? He came to the earth, the second greatest of God's inanimate creations.

Here on this earth God said I am going to create man

in my own image. It doesn't mean that God has arms and legs but knowledge, personality, will. Man, the creature of God made in the image of God. And so Lucifer, banished from heaven came to earth and turned himself into Satan, and he continues the war of rebellion against God through God's creatures. He has only one thing in mind and that is to create a life-style, a society, a world, totally devoid of anything which bespeaks authority or control.

And so he came to Adam and Eve with a proposition. He said that God is withholding from your good. God doesn't want you to be happy. God is your enemy. He is against you. All these laws: do this, and don't do that— are to confine you and make life miserable. If you would only do what you wanted to do, if you would eat the fruit anyway, you would be a god. You see, kick over the traces. God is against you. To be under his control and to be his servant is to be miserable. The way to really fly is to let 'er rip. Just do anything you want to do. You see, that is Satan's only offer. That is all he's got. That's his bag, his program. All he wants is to create a world in which there is no control and man is free to be his own god.

Down through history, man has lived with the principle of sin in him. In the deepest part of every believer, of every Christian, let alone of every non-Christian, the mystery of iniquity, the principle of evil, the principle of sin which wants to create a life-style devoid of control where man is himself God exists.

Just beneath the veneer of the finest Christian there is always the still small subtle voice that says: "If only I could do what I think, if only I could do what I really want to do. But no, I'll not do it, I will do what I am supposed to do." But it is always there.

Now, for the first time in history, we have a generation of young men and women who are able to do anything they want to. Now it is possible to have a life-style in which anything goes. Within six blocks of our church in downtown Houston for five dollars you can do or see anything you can think of. Anything the mind can see or imagine or conceive can be bought and paid for and done in five minutes. So what has happened? Now the illusion has shattered. The mask has been ripped off. The bubble has burst. And a generation of people who have believed that if they could do what they want to do, they would be happy, now have been able to do it, and guess what? *They're not happy.*

We have a generation of the most bewildered and confused and frustrated young men and women this world has ever seen. The devil's lie has been exposed. They can do what they want and by eighteen, or nineteen, they have popped all their corks and blown all their fuses, and busted all their gaskets, and are over the hill at twenty-one. They're flat, they are pooped out and popped out and burnt out and they are empty and frustrated and they have done it all. And it didn't produce the panacea it purported to propose and they are empty and frustrated and bewildered and confused and hungry.

Into the vacuum that has been left is rushing every kind of eastern religion and demonology and witchcraft and occult and heresy imaginable. Yet this very philosophy of iniquity in which man has done his own thing has also created the greatest possible spiritual awakening in the history of the world. Now toward the end of time we do have the parallel, increase, strengthening and emerging and unifying of both of these philosophies. And, indeed, one has served as a catalyst to trigger off the other. The Jesus Movement is sweeping the nation and Campus Crusade and Youth for Christ and a hundred other good things are sweeping the country and kids are being turned on to Jesus by the tens and hundreds of thousands. The Jesus Movement is real. It is on. And the church is standing by scratching its head trying to figure out what is happening and saying we didn't think it up. We didn't program it. So it must not be right.

If the church does not spend money and start programs and go on the offensive immediately to win as many as possible—to rush in to this vacuum with the truth about Christ it runs the danger of missing the greatest chance for evangelism the world has ever seen. Man, it's now. It's hot. Revival never has been as possible. It's never been as ready. It has never been as easy as it is now! Now you say, preacher, what is going to happen? Lucifer declared war on Christ. He said I'm taking over the world. And that battle cry, that ultimatum is going to be resolved. The showdown is going to come in Armageddon.

Three things have to happen leading up to that:

1. The nation, the world has to become preoccupied with an obsession against law. It has been submerged, it has been hidden and covered. Satan, knowing his days are numbered, that he is fast emerging toward the unification of all the evil forces of the world in conflict against all the Christian forces in Armageddon is ripping off his mask of disguise and is going to become increasingly obnoxious and repulsive and open and blatant in his attack.

Any psychologist will tell you that a child grows up with an image of God in what he sees in his father. His father is the god image to him. And there are other things as we go through life that are images of God. You see God is the original and consummate authority image in the world. And as man tries to get back the original proposition of creating a world without any control, he begins to attack everything which bespeaks control.

Everything today which slightly stands for control and discipline is under attack. Down with the preacher, down with the flag, down with school. I asked a bunch of kids on campus the other day, "What are you going to take next year?" and they said, "The administration building." Down with the professor and the Bible and the cop on the beat and the soldier and the court.

To me, whether you are for or against capital punish-

ment or legalized marijuana or abortion is not really that
important. But what is important is that it is a symptom
which the Christian must understand of a far deeper
problem. And that is that every law and every discipli-
nary philosophy is going to come under attack. Who says
I cannot take another man's life and get away with it?
Who is going to tell me what I can smoke and can't? Who
is going to tell me that I cannot have control over my
own body? Who says I have to pay taxes? Who says a
woman can't be raped? Who says I can't rob a bank?
What right do you have to tell me that I have to stop if
the sign is red?

We haven't seen anything yet. We are going to see an
increasing open assault on the court, the Presidency, the
Senate, the police, the mayor, the flag, the judicial system, the jail system—anything that tells me that there are
some things that I cannot do. But it is only a symptom
of a basic strengthening emerging, unifying life-style of
man against the ultimate authority over his life which is
God. And the believer *must* understand what is happening in his world.

Many a young person who is going into social work
and who is planning to be a psychologist and sociologist,
who is primarily going to be dealing with trying to pick
up the pieces, should be giving themselves to become
missionaries and evangelists and going to the source of
the problem. Many of you need to redirect your life-style
and your life commitment. Back in the old days before

we got so high-faluting, they used to have a simple test to determine whether a man was sane or crazy. They would put him in a little room and lock the door and give him a bucket and a mop. They would plug up the sink and turn on the water and let it run over. Well, if the old boy had sense enough to go over and turn off the water he was sane and they let him out. But if he spent all of his time trying to mop up the slop and pick up the water out of the bucket and didn't go to the source, he was too crazy to turn loose on society. We have got an awful lot of programs and approaches that are doing nothing except dealing with the symptom. I am saying that there is an urgency with which the church and her young people and her leaders must commit themselves to aggressive, evangelistic, world action now.

And so before the end can come, three things have to happen. First, lawlessness will emerge and unify. It will increase and our obsession to legalize marijuana, abolish capital punishment, legalize abortion, and all of these things are only forerunners of what is going to happen. For the devil will become increasingly blatant in his attack against anything which tells anybody he cannot do anything. Now the second thing that has to happen is that God's patience will be exhausted with man's rebellion. Now the Bible tells us in 1 Thessalonians that one of these days God is going to look down on this earth and say "That's enough—get my church out of that filthy world."

Let me ask you this. What is the only factor in the
world which holds back sin and keeps immorality in
check? It is the Holy Spirit. He is the moral conscience
of government. He is the moral conscience of society.
He is the moral conscience of the man in the street. He
is the only influence in force that keeps sin in check as
much as it is. Now, in whom is the Holy Spirit? He is not
in books, in buildings, in desks, in pianos. He is in the
hearts of the believer. He is in Christians.

One of these days God is going to get enough and he
is going to say, "Get my church out of this sinful, filthy,
rebellious, rotten world. Take them away." And the rapture of the church is going to occur. Christians will be
taken away and the Holy Spirit will be taken out of the
world. *Then the world is going to get what it has always really
wanted. All the sin it wants!* And it is going to be so "hella-
cious," so awful, the Bible says men will have great running sores, there will be disease and rebellion and war
and filth.

Life without God, life without restraint, life without
the church, without discipline, without control, life without the believer, the salt of the earth being removed, the
meat will so putrify and rot that men will cry to God.
They will beg for the rocks and mountains to fall on them
and kill them and destroy them. But it won't happen.
Death will flee from them.

Then in the resultant confusion someone is going to
step forward. He will be very handsome, very intelligent,

very attractive, very powerful and he will have a platform. The papers and TV will herald him as the new Messiah. He will be the son of perdition. Satan incarnate in a man. Antichrist! He will be swept into office, swept into power. The world will be unified under him. The world will honor him. His platform is going to be the mystery of iniquity. His whole philosophy will be that the reason for the problems of the world is because there have been laws and control. "Let's create a world with no laws," he'll say. And the world will say, "Yes, that's wonderful." A world with no law, no court, no policeman. Do your own thing.

That is today at the grassroots of society. Today it is emerging. Now, understand before one man can step forward and get hold of things in the confusion created by the removal of the Holy Spirit and the people of God, the world is going to have to be in a state that is easily unifiable. Today we have telstar. One man can address the whole world live, visually, simultaneously. Do we see any other signs of unity in the world? The United States government is getting ready to spend millions to get us on the metric system where things are measured by meters, not yards and feet. One common world system of measurement. We are moving toward one common world language. One world court. One world police force. One world monetary system, with the pound as the universal measure of buying and selling. You see it all around the world. Unity. Unity. So that one person can take over the entire world.

In the book of Luke Jesus was promised to reign on the throne of his father David. The Bible says in Luke 1:32–33 that Jesus Christ will come and reign on the throne of the temple of his father David. He must reign. But before Jesus comes and stands on the Mount of Olives and attempts to assume that throne, antichrist will have taken the throne and he will say that he is god. And the world will worship him. Right there is where the water hits the wheel and Jesus says, "No, I am God. I will take the throne."

The battle of Armageddon occurs in the Valley of Megiddo, around the hills of Jerusalem, with Jerusalem as the prize. There the world's ultimate question is going to be resolved. Who is going to be God? Whose world is this? The kingdoms of this world will become the kingdom of our God and his Son. Second Thessalonians 2:3–7 says:

> "Let no man deceive you by any means: for that day" [that day means the coming of Christ always in Scripture] "for that day shall not come, except there come a falling away first, and that man of sin" [the antichrist, that is] "be revealed, the son of perdition; who opposeth and exalteth himself above all that is called God, or that is worshipped; so that he as God sitteth in the temple of God, showing himself that he is God. Remember ye not, that, when I was

yet with you, I told you these things? And now ye know what withholdeth that he might be revealed in his time. For the mystery of iniquity" [this principle of sin, this rising attitude in society of do your own thing] "doth already work: only he who now letteth will let, until he be taken out of the way."

The word "let" means restrain or hold back. Who holds it in check? Who holds evil back? Who holds Satan back? The Holy Spirit, and he will continue to do so until he be taken out of the way at the rapture of the church.

"And then shall that Wicked be revealed," [then will antichrist be exposed, assuming the temple and saying I am the Messiah, I am the Christ, I am God] "whom the Lord shall consume with the spirit of his mouth, and shall destroy with the brightness of his coming" (v. 8). In the battle of Armageddon when all the forces of evil are unified under antichrist, and all the forces of righteousness shall come and all the angels with him and the saints, redeemed of God in the battle of Armageddon, there is not going to be a shot fired. And yet the blood will be so deep in the valley that it will run to the bits of the horses mouths.

The kingdom of Satan is a kingdom of darkness, and the coming of Jesus will be with such great brightness and lightness and white purity that they will be blinded. They cannot stand the brightness of his coming and in the resulting confusion I believe the forces of antichrist in their chaos and confusion will turn and destroy each other. They will all be consumed. How? With a gun, with a battle, with a fight, with a helicopter? No! With the brightness of his coming!

"Even him, whose coming is after the working of Satan" (that is antichrist) "with all power and signs and lying wonders. And with all deceivableness of unrighteousness in them that perish; because they received not the love of the truth, that they might be saved" (vv. 9–10). You see, they refused to believe the truth and be saved, so here is what is going to happen. "And for this cause" [because the world refused to be saved, refused to believe the truth] "God shall send them strong delusion, that they should believe a lie" (v. 11).

Remember when God hardened Pharaoh's heart? I have heard preachers try to preach around that. There is no way you can get around that. God *did* harden Pharaoh's heart. He couldn't believe if he wanted to. God locked him in his sin; he locked him in his hardened heart; he locked him in the sin of blindness and unbelief. But he gave him ten chances to repent first. And because the world refused to believe Christ, believe the truth, God said if that is what you want I will send you delusion. I'll lock you in your darkness. I'll lock you in your blindness. I'll lock you in your sin and unbelief. So that they all might be damned. Because you believe not the truth and you have pleasure in unrighteousness.

Recentiy my wife and I were standing on the Mount

of Olives in the Holy Land. Now there are two problems that I have had. One, the Bible says in Zechariah that when the Messiah comes back to the earth he shall stand on the Mount of Olives. And the Mount of Olives shall cleave to the north and to the south, and fall from the east to the west. That means that when he touches it, when the Messiah comes to the Mount of Olives, it is going to split in half and fall apart. I didn't understand that. Why? Another problem that I have had is that the Temple where Jesus is going to reign which antichrist will have assumed in fulfilment of prophesy, on that temple site—there is no temple there! It is today the site of a Muslim mosque. So that thing has got to be destroyed. It has got to go before they can rebuild the temple there.

Incidentally, our guide told us that it is reputed in Israel today that the Jews are already digging and excavating secretly the foundation of the new temple. It is also rumored that they are making certain stones for the new temple. It is going to be built!

What does it mean, that the Mount of Olives is going to split? How are we going to get rid of that Muslim mosque, where the temple of King David must be built, so that the Messiah can come and reign on it? Let's back up a minute. When man fell, when sin began, you remember that the Bible says that the earth fell too. There were no thorns in the roses, no weeds in the fields. The Bible says all of the earth groaneth awaiting its redemption. The earthquakes, the underground cave-ins, the mine disasters, the earth groaning, preparing for the day it will be remade. The Bible says that at the end of the world, the heavens and the earth will dissolve, elements will melt and pass away, with fervent heat. He is going to make it all over again, a new heaven and a new earth.

In the last days, the Bible says, there are going to be earthquakes in diverse places. The whole earth is going to be shifting in preparation of the day when it will dissolve and become a new heaven and a new earth, a new society and a new social order that will be instituted, not by McGovern, not by Nixon, not by the United Nations, not by the Peace Corps, but peace by the Prince of Peace. So what is going to happen? I theorize simply that the Temple, the present Muslim mosque is going to be shattered and destroyed by these earthquakes. And in that same earthquake will split the Mount of Olives.

We stood at the Mount of Olives and saw that in the floor of the valley to the south the way that it goes, if it were to keep right on coming right through that mountain, it would split in half. Geologists today verify the existence of a fault at the bottom of the Mountain of Olives. So that very same earthquake, to me in all likeliness, which destroys the temple so that a new one can be built will also crack the Mount of Olives, coming right up the basin of that canyon. It will split but not quite fall in half so that when Jesus Christ and the saints come, when they stand on that precarious balance, it will fall.

Then Jesus will march right down that mountain and across the valley, through the Eastern Gate and assume the throne of the Temple, and the kingdoms of the world will become the kingdoms of our God and his Son.

The kingdoms of education and entertainment and society and sociology, the kingdom of medicine, the kingdom of finance, as well as the political kingdoms of the world will all become the kingdoms of our God and his Son.

Let me say this in closing, people say to me, "Preacher, is there life on other planets?" I don't know. But I do know this. If there is, it is not a higher type life than we have here on this earth. They would not be ahead of us. Why? Because man is made in the image of God, and you just can't do any better than that. That is just about as high up as you can get. No, they are not any higher type than we are.

The earth before the Pleistocene Age was an equatorial paradise made for man in the image of a beautiful God. It was all perfect. And God had planned a society that would honor him and be a showcase for the universe, to see what it would be like when a group of people, made in the image of God would honor him. The will of God, though deferred, will ultimately be done. This world is going to honor Christ. That is why he made it. Man will honor Jesus. This earth is going to honor Christ. So then, every knee shall bow and every tongue confess that Christ is Lord.

"All hail the power of Jesus name! Let angels prostrate fall. Bring forth the royal diadem, And crown him Him Lord of all." This world is not out of control. God has a plan. He is very much in control of that plan. The second coming of Christ is that one central event of history toward which all of history is moving and without which none in history makes any sense.

Jean Paul Sarte said, "Society is in a room without windows. There is no exit from the human dilemma." Before his death, Secretary of the United Nations, Dag Hammarskjöld, said, "We have tried so hard and failed so miserably, there is no possibility of world peace." But they are wrong. This world will be a perfect world. There will be peace. The kingdoms of the world will become kingdoms of our Lord, Jesus Christ. Before that can be done, the ultimate battle, the ultimate settling of the original declaration of war by Lucifer on Jesus for the control of the world and the question who's going to be God has to be settled.

When Jesus reigns and there is a thousand year's peace on this earth before there is a new heaven and a new earth he will reign on the throne of his Father David in Jerusalem. There will be peace in the valley. The bear and the lion and the lamb shall lay down by each other. There will be harmony and peace among men.

Can we, as Christians, understanding that the movement of history, so cateclismically close, so dynamically concluding about us, so grand and glorious, and so near, can we stand idly by and not be moving in conquest into those open vacuums with the gospel of Jesus? I beg of you, in Jesus' name, that you pay the price, that you make the commitment, that you gear up as teachers and deacons and soul-winners. Young people in the campus and in the schools rush in with your witness and with your testimony—anything and everything you have—to bring men to Jesus Christ and into the kingdom of God while there is time, for our Lord is coming soon.